GRANUAILE
THE LIFE AND TIMES OF
GRACE O'MALLEY
c. 1530–1603

From the reviews of the first edition:

'While Granuaile is a well established legendary figure it was left to Ms Chambers to present us with a historical reality which is equally if not more compelling than the legend.'

Sunday Tribune

'A superbly researched work . . . it salvages the 16th century Mistress of the Western Waves from the rather frivolous folklore which surrounds her.'

Irish Times

'Chambers depicts the history and way of life in 16th century Connaught in a scholarly and informing manner.'

Irish Independent

'. . . a fascinating and wide-ranging book, extensive and valuable, and to be welcomed.'

Irish Press

'For sheer, meticulous research, it would be hard to beat Anne Chambers.'

Dungarvan Observer

'. . . detached, authoritative . . . and full of fascinating highlights.'

Image

'. . . the book reaches out and draws Granuaile in from the vagueness. It presents us with a person — an incredible person, but a person who was part of factual history.'

Ireland's Own

'. . . an excellent compendium of diligent research, and provides both facts and sources about a period of Irish history which, although already very thoroughly studied by historians and novelists, still provides new insights and understanding for the determined student of the times.'

Irish Press

'. . . a lively readable account of the life of this remarkable woman . . . presents a clear picture of life in Ireland during the sixteenth century with its occasional barbarity contrasting with an unusual refinement.

Mayo News

'. . . well worth reading as background to Irish life at the time which set the stage for every event in our history from that day to this. It's a model of research, well-produced and annotated, and the kind of book that every researcher would like to write.'

Bookweek, RTE Radio 1

'This book should be available in every history classroom as the author is adept at giving 20th century readers a flavour of 16th century Ireland. The illustrations, appendices, bibliography and index are excellent.'

Cork Examiner

'Anyone who has tried to find out any substantial information on Grace O'Malley will know that a good basic book on this subject has long been needed. Ms Chambers has filled this gap with what will probably remain the standard work on Granuaile for some time.'

The Irish Post

GRANUAILE

The Life and Times of Grace O'Malley
c. 1530–1603

A New and Revised Edition

Anne Chambers

WOLFHOUND PRESS
Celebrating 25 *Years*

This edition first published in 1998 by
Wolfhound Press Ltd
68 Mountjoy Square
Dublin 1, Ireland
Tel: (353-1) 874 0354
Fax: (353-1) 872 0207

Published in the US and Canada by
The Irish American Book Company
6309 Monarch Park Place
Niwot, Colorado 80503
USA
Tel: (303) 652-2710
Fax: (303) 652-2689

First edition published in hardback 1979
First paperback edition 1983. Reprinted 1986
New edition 1988. Reprinted 1991, 1994

Wolfhound Press receives financial assistance from the Arts Council/
An Chomhairle Ealaíon, Dublin, Ireland.

British Library Cataloguing in Publication Data
A catalogue record for this book is available from the British Library.

ISBN 0-86327-631-8

10 9 8 7 6 5 4 3

Cover Photograph: Slide File
Cover Design: Slick Fish Design
Typesetting: Wolfhound Press
Printed and bound by The Guernsey Press Co. Ltd, Guernsey, Channel
Islands.

Contents

In memory of my grandfather,
JAMES CRUISE

List of Illustrations

Acknowledgements

National Library of Ireland
Public Record Office of Ireland
Genealogical Office of Ireland
Celtic Studies Department, UCD
Royal Irish Academy
Trinity College Library
National Monuments Section, Office of Public Works, Dublin
Public Record Office, London
Lambeth Palace Library, London
Hatfield House Library, Herts.
Lord Sligo, Westport House
Mr Gaisford St Lawrence, Howth Castle
Ms Máirín Ní Dhomhnalláin
Mr Kenneth Nicholls, UCC
Mr Jonathan Williams
Mr Michael Bevan
Wolfhound Press

Author's Note

It is almost twenty years since the first edition of *Granuaile, The Life and Times of Grace O'Malley* was published. Since 1979 the book has been in constant print, and the popularity of the subject has been reflected in its success.

I can honestly say that every year since, I have become involved in some project about Granuaile. Documentaries for TV and radio, innumerable articles for books and magazines, interviews and lectures, dance dramas, musicals and ballads, Shaun Davey's evocative *Granuaile Suite*, an interpretative centre based on her life and times, the launch of a new ferry bearing her name, a feature film screenplay — the number and range of undertakings associated with her seem never-ending. Granuaile seems to have captured the imagination of everyone who reads about her, just as she captured mine.

Over the years I have come to realise how much I owe her. It is fair to say that she has changed my life, leading me on my own voyage of self-discovery, making me abandon one career midstream for the precarious life of a writer, sending me halfway around the world to tell her story from Connemara to Kingston, introducing me to people in every walk of life — many, through her, have become friends.

It is in an effort to repay this undoubted debt that I have embarked on this new edition of her biography. There are, however, also more practical reasons for writing it. *Granuaile* was my first book. After twenty years and some half-dozen books under my 'quill', I feel that I may have honed away sufficiently at whatever writing skill I possess to attempt to do justice to her story. With the passing years I have got to know and perhaps understand Granuaile more than I did, and am less in awe and more in empathy with her now.

Since 1979 I have had access to some additional information

relating to her, particularly among the manuscripts in the Westport House collection, and also in the archives of public institutions such as the Public Record Office, the Royal Irish Academy and the Department of Celtic Studies, UCD. I found additional information also among the English State Papers of the period, not least another petition of hers written in 1595.

Combined with these new revelations, I wanted to re-examine and analyse, in a more comprehensive way, her life and the contribution she made to her time. I wanted especially to examine her life in the context of women's role in history, both political and social, as well as the relationship between women and the sea (so much part of both the fact and the legend of Granuaile), which still remains a male bastion, as little encroached upon by modern-day woman as it was in the time of Granuaile.

And what emerges with greater clarity and assurance than ever is the life of a truly unique and remarkable mould-breaker — a woman far more liberated and empowered than any in this age of perceived equality, with its female heads of state and astronauts, corporate businesswomen and women legislators, not to mention the girl-power motivation of the Spice Girls. Perhaps most intriguing of all is the fact that Granuaile managed to compete and succeed within the male-dominated environment in which she operated without jettisoning her femininity. Her success and notoriety were not achieved at the expense of her womanhood. On the contrary, she maximised and utilised her feminine attributes and enjoyed the pleasures her womanhood conferred through her marriage(s), motherhood and sexual fulfilment — surely the exemplification of a true feminist.

Anne Chambers
Dublin, 1998

Introduction

> There came to me also a most famous feminine sea captain
> called Granny Imallye and offered her services unto me, wher-
> esoever I would command her, with three galleys and two
> hundred fighting men, either in Scotland or Ireland. She
> brought with her her husband for she was as well by sea as by
> land well more than Mrs Mate with him. . . . This was a notori-
> ous woman in all the coasts of Ireland.
>
> *Sir Henry Sidney, Lord Deputy of Ireland, 1576*

This tantalising cameo is one of many descriptions in the Elizabethan state papers of a most remarkable Irishwoman. This
'notorious woman' provoked awe, anger, revulsion, admiration
and pity in the sixteenth-century English administrators and
military men who, by persuasion and by the sword, came to
conquer the land of her birth. But in Ireland for over four hundred years she was destined to remain a prisoner of indiffer-
ence, as Irish history chose to ignore the unique contribution
she made to the social, political and maritime history of her
time. However, folklore, poetry and fiction showed no such
bias and must be congratulated for preserving the memory of
one of the most remarkable women of history, Grainne
O'Malley, or as she is more familiarly known in Ireland,
Granuaile.

Like her sisters, Granuaile was a victim of the mainly male
orientation of historical record and analysis. But in her case
more than mere male chauvinism ensured her dismissal from
the pages of history. By not fitting the mould determined and
demanded by later generations of Irish historians, Granuaile
committed an additional transgression. Until relatively recently,
Irish heroes and heroines were required to be suitably adorned
in the green cloak of patriotism, their personal lives untainted,
their religious beliefs fervently Roman Catholic, with an

occasional allowance made for 'rebel Protestants'. Granuaile was, as one of her male detractors wrote of her, 'a woman who overstepped the part of womanhood'.[1] In not allowing religious, social or political convention to deter her during her lifetime, she did not readily fit the required mould.

There are many aspects of her life that could qualify her as *persona non grata* in the roll-call of Irish heroes. She brazenly superseded her husband in his anointed role as chieftain, thereby contravening the Salic law on which Gaelic succession was based. She assumed personal command of her father's fleet of galleys and was accepted as undisputed leader, living in close proximity with her hardbitten all-male sailors. She traded and pirated successfully for the space of fifty years from Ireland to Scotland, possibly as far afield as Spain. She led rebellions against individual English administrators when they tried to curb her activities, yet allied with the Queen of England when it was to her political advantage. She attacked her own son when he dared to side with her enemy, trained another son so well in the art of survival that he fought with the English forces at the Battle of Kinsale, the last stand of the Gaelic world that bred and bore her. Granuaile allowed neither social nor political convention to deter her ambition. She took a lover, divorced a husband, gave birth to her youngest son on board her ship at sea, made no distinction as to nationality when plundering Irish, English or Spanish ships. Granuaile, the 'chief commander and director of thieves and murderers at sea',[2] hardly fitted the rosy-hued picture of Gaelic womanhood painted by latter-day male and often clerical historians.

Her role in the history of the sixteenth century was allowed lapse into the realm of folklore and fiction. It is ironic that there is no mention of her name in the *Annals of the Four Masters* — that seminal source of Irish history, compiled shortly after her death, and in a place where memories of her activities were still verdant. The English state papers, on the other hand, contain references to her as late as 1627, some twenty-four years after her death. Such bias erased from the pages of Irish history one of the most remarkable women of the past and by so doing diminished our understanding of the period.

However, it is a measure of Granuaile's greatness that her

memory at least was preserved by legend and by lore. Legends are not created about insignificant people. To be remembered in folk memory is as much a tribute to the impact she made in her life as any academic treatise. As to the factual evidence, it was left to her contemporary English administrators and generals in Ireland to record aspects of the extraordinary role she played. These Elizabethan documents are now faded and brittle, their age-darkened, spider-like handwriting evidence of the passage of four hundred years since their authors put quill to parchment. But from the swirls and flourishes of the sixteenth-century scribes the story of Grainne O'Malley springs to life. When the factual evidence relating to her life is examined within the context of the traumatic times in which she lived, she emerges as a fearless leader, by land and by sea, a political pragmatist and tactician, a ruthless plunderer, a mercenary, a part-time rebel, a shrewd and able negotiator, and, above all, a woman who broke the mould and played a unique role in history.

The story of Granuaile is the story of one remarkable woman's quest for survival and fulfilment by land and sea, in a time of profound political upheaval and male chauvinistic bias.

Granuaile's Connaught.

1

Powerful by Land and Sea

Duine maith riamh ní raibh
D'iabh Máille acht 'n a mháraidhe;
Fáidhe na síne sibh-sí,
Dine baidhe is bhraithirrí.

A good man never was there
Of the O'Malleys but a mariner,
The prophets of the weather are ye,
A hospitable and brotherly clan.

O'Dugan (d. 1372)

Granuaile was born into the clan Uí Mháille, a hardy, seafaring people on the west coast of Ireland. According to the ancient genealogies of Ireland, the O'Malleys were descended from the eldest son of a High King of Ireland, Brian Orbsen, who was killed at the battle of Dam Chluain, near Tuam, Co. Galway, circa AD 388. They were hereditary lords of the region called the Umhalls (umhall meaning territory), later anglicised as the Owles, a territory which comprised the baronies of Murrisk on the south shore of Clew Bay and Burrishoole on the north. The barony of Murrisk, called Umhall Uachtarach or Upper Owle included the islands of Clare, Inishturk, Caher, Inishbofin, Inishark and a multitude of smaller islands within Clew Bay. The barony of Burrishoole was called Umhall Iochtarach, or Lower Owle, and originally included the island of Achill. The two baronies were generally referred to as 'Umhall Uí Mháille' (territory of the O'Malleys) or the Owles.

In 1235, however, the Anglo-Norman De Burgos invaded Connaught and in a great demonstration of military power swept aside the fragmented Gaelic opposition. In the transition of land and power that followed, the Botiller or Butlers were granted some of the O'Malley territory of Umhall Iochtarach, the barony of Burrishoole, known as Leath Fherghuis, Fergus's half — Fergus being head of one of the three O'Malley septs. They built a castle there known as Tyrenmore, near Burrishoole Abbey. The Butlers in turn were later dispossessed by the sept of Ulick de Burgo, but Achill reverted back to the O'Malleys.

The O'Malleys lived in relative harmony with their de Burgo neighbours, becoming their allies in war. In 1342, the de Burgos, like many of their fellow Anglo-Normans, renounced their allegiance to the English crown and adopted Gaelic names and customs. They divided into two branches, the Mayo Bourses who adopted the title MacWilliam Iochtarach (the Lower Mac William) and the Galway Burkes who became known as the MacWilliam Uachtarach (the upper MacWilliam). It appears that they had the approval of the O'Malley chieftain who gave his daughter Sabina in marriage to the new MacWilliam of Mayo. Unlike the other sub-chieftains under the MacWilliam, the O'Malley chieftain paid no rent in tribute to his powerful overlord, but merely a 'rising out of six score bands to be maintained by himself, but they have maintenance for the first night from MacWilliam.'[1]

The earliest written reference to the O'Malley territory of Umhall is in association with the ascent by St Patrick in the fifth century of the spectacular conical mountain then known as Cruachan Aigle (Eagle Mountain). In Tireacháin's note on the life of the saint, contained in the *Book of Armagh*, was written:

> And Patrick went to Mount Egli to fast on it for forty days and forty nights, keeping the discipline of Moses, Elias and Christ. And his charioteer died in Muirisc Aigli, that is the plain between the sea and Aicill and he buried the charioteer, Totmael, and piled stones as a sepulchre. . . .[2]

Patrick's pilgrimage in AD 441 is commemorated annually by thousands of people who walk in his footsteps to the summit of the mountain that now bears his name.

Clew Bay.

The rugged, scenic splendour of the Umhalls moved William Makepeace Thackeray to write in 1842: 'It forms an event in one's life to have seen that place, so beautiful is it and so unlike all other beauties that I know of.'[3] The territory is encompassed by the towering peak of Croagh Patrick to the south, Mweelrea, Croaghmore on Clare Island, Slievemore on Achill to the west, and the Nephin range to the north. At its heart is the broad expanse of the island-strewn Clew Bay, that 'miracle of beauty', with Clare Island, a Sphinx-like bulwark against the surge of the wild Atlantic ocean that stretches away towards the western horizon. The Umhalls comprised some fertile areas around Belclare and Murrisk, and wide tracts of bog, marsh, rough mountain grazing and extensive woodland. Apart from its scenic beauty, this sea-washed territory of the Umhalls was an appropriate base for a seafaring clan.

Although an island, Ireland has produced few seafaring families of note. The O'Malleys differed from the great majority of Irish clans in that they derived their living mainly from the sea. Their clan motto, *'terra marique potens'* (powerful by land and sea) proclaimed them lords of the seas around Ireland. In the ancient *Book of Rights* (*Leabhar na gCeart*), which lists the rights and tributes paid to the King of Connaught, it is recorded: 'the command of the fleet to O'Flaherti and O'Mali, whenever he (the king) goes on sea or on the high sea'.[4] O'Malley paid the King at his residence at Cruachan a yearly tribute of 'one hundred milch cows, one hundred hogs and one hundred casks of beer'. The King, in return for O'Malley's service, tributes and loyalty, presented him with the substantial annual gift of 'five ships, five horses, five swords and five corselets'.[5]

Like many coastal families, the O'Malleys claimed a traditional lordship of their immediate sea territory, which included the levying of tolls for right of passage and the selling of fishing rights to others, especially foreigners. Writing in 1579, one English administrator sought to abolish this custom:

> Towards the sea coast there lieth many fair islands, rich and plentiful of all commodities, there cometh hither every year likely about fifty English ships for fishing. They have been compelled to pay a great tribute to the O'Malleys. . . .[6]

But unlike most coastal families, the O'Malleys were themselves intrepid seafarers, whose seafaring was not confined to Ireland. A verse of a fifteenth-century poem confirms what tradition also maintained — that they traded and plundered as far as Spain and Scotland.

> *Leomhain an oirir uaine*
> *eolaigh oirir na Spáinne*
> *ag buain chruidh do Ceann Tíre*
> *gearr míle ar muir d'ibh Máille*

> They are the lions of the green sea
> men acquainted with the land of Spain
> when seizing cattle from Cantyre,
> a mile by sea is a short distance to the O'Malleys.[7]

In 1123, the name Uí Máille appears in the *Annals of the Four Masters*, which records that 'Tadhg Ua Máille lord of Umhall was drowned with his ship at Aran.'[8] From then the name appears frequently, usually in connection with the clan's seafaring exploits. In 1413 the annals record how when Tuathal O'Malley was returning home from mercenary service in Ulster,

> with seven ships and their crews . . . a storm arose on the western sea, which drove them to the right towards Scotland, where six of the ships, with all their crews were sunk . . . Tuathal himself with much difficulty effected a landing in Scotland.[9]

The annals state that 244 of Tuathal's crewmen were drowned in the tragedy, an indication of his substantial following and seapower. It was the same Tuathal O'Malley who, on being wounded in a quarrel with a poet, instead of claiming an eric (the legal payment for bloodshed), chose instead to have the poet compose for him a poem. In his bardic verses, the poet eulogised Tuathal and praised him for his choice:

> You did not claim a pledge for your wound
> You ignored the loss of the best blood
> Here to requite you for it is a melodious poem
> You deserved from me the price of your healing.[10]

It required a special measure of skill and daring to extract a living from the sea along the formidable Atlantic seaboard. The sea routes north to Scotland and south to the Continent, along the indented western coastline, were hazardous. They were made even more so by impediments such as basic navigational aids, the absence of well-defined charts, wooden-hulled ships and the ever-present threat of piracy. But their mobility by sea gave the O'Malleys distinct advantages over their landbound neighbours. It provided them with an escape route from their enemies in time of attack, an advantage availed of later both by Granuaile and her sons. It allowed them access to foreign markets to sell their produce in exchange for goods unavailable at home. It is reasonable to assume that over the centuries O'Malley castles were bedecked with more exotic furnishings than their neighbours and their table replenished with the wines of France and Spain. Less tangible, but nonetheless advantageous, was an opportunity denied most of their landbound contemporaries — to mingle with other peoples and cultures, to observe, to learn, to glean knowledge of events in the wider world outside Ireland. To seafaring folk like the O'Malleys, the sea was ever a highway, while landlubbers saw it only as a barrier.

Recent research on trade links between Ireland and the Continent has confirmed that which tradition has always held — that from the Middle Ages, Irish-owned ships, manned by Irish crews, regularly crossed the seas to ports in England, France and Spain. The ports along the west coast of Ireland tended to trade with Bristol in England, ports on the west coast of France and on the coast of Galicia in northern Spain. For a seagoing clan like the O'Malleys, there was another incentive for them to trade their produce in foreign markets. Galway city was the centre of trade on the west coast and by the early sixteenth century was described as 'one of the first emporia of trade, not only in Ireland, but with few exceptions, in the British isles as well'.[11] But the wealthy merchant rulers of the city had enacted a series of restrictive by-laws prohibiting non-residents, particularly the Gaelic clans outside the city walls, from trading there. Trade in wool, the mainstay of many Gaelic clans, was prohibited. In 1460, the Corporation had enacted:

> that ne merchent, ne maryner, ne shipman, should unlode, ne transport over the seas, unfremans goods, but only fremans, upon paine to lesse the said goods or the just value therof and to forfoyte 100 shillings.[12]

A by-law of 1518 fined citizens who entertained their Gaelic neighbours within the city without licence of the mayor and council on any feastday so 'that neither O' ne Mac shall strutte ne swagger thru the streets of Galway'.[13] Taxes on trading within the city, coupled with the racist sentiment of the by-law, made it imperative for the O'Malleys to sail with their produce, free from taxes and restrictions, to foreign markets, from their own ports of Burrishoole and Clare Island.

Fishing was one of the clan's main sources of income. The fishing grounds off the coast of O'Malley's lordship were considered among the most fertile in Ireland. Herring was the principal species caught, with hake, cod, ling, turbot, salmon and shellfish. The fish was usually salted, sometimes dried, and packed in wooden barrels for export. Hides, tallow, frieze cloth, deer and sheepskins, furs such as pinemarten (considered a highly fashionable accessory in the sixteenth century), coney, fox and otter were other important commodities from the west of Ireland which found a ready market abroad.

Fishing, however, was not the sole maritime activity of the clan. As in most coastal communities, plundering and piracy had supplemented the O'Malley income from earliest times. The ancient annals record with regular monotony O'Malley raids on outlying coastal settlements from Kerry to Donegal.

> Eogan O'Maille went with the crews of three ships against Cille bega [Killybegs, Co. Donegal] in the night. . . . They raid and burn the town and take many prisoners.[14]

Granuaile, who indulged in the profession with more success than perhaps any of her ancestors, was accused of being 'a chief director and commander of thieves and murderers at sea',[15] and raided from Scotland to the south coast of Ireland.

Piracy has been in existence for over five thousand years, from ancient Persia to modern-day China. Every known civilisation through the ages has produced a pirate community. Depending on mainly political and, to a lesser degree, cultural considerations, piracy has been viewed pragmatically by rulers down through the centuries. 'The Ancient Greeks and Carthaginians had no qualms about piracy being proper conduct.'[16] The Vikings used it as a means of establishing footholds in Ireland, Britain and the Continent. In the Red Sea, the Persian Gulf and all along the north African coast, piracy flourished throughout history. In the Far East it was undertaken on a massive scale and still exists today. Granuaile's great contemporary, Queen Elizabeth I, gave her letters of marque to the pirate turned privateer, Sir Francis Drake, when it seemed likely that his unlawful activities on the high seas would substantially supplement her state coffers. Despite their notoriety, it is worth noting that Granuaile's career predated by one hundred and fifty years the careers of the more widely known Caribbean women pirates, the Irish-born Ann Bonny, and her companion, Mary Read.

Galway City, 1611.

The struggle for power and profit at sea no more than mirrored a similar struggle on land, but perhaps had more romance and notoriety. Piracy is often a symptom of political chaos on land, and in Ireland in the sixteenth century, as the old Gaelic world faced the ultimate assault by a more powerful neighbour and slowly disintegrated, this was very obviously the case. This period saw Granuaile's career at sea reach its zenith. Her strongholds were situated deep within the inlets of Clew Bay, inaccessible to any but those with a local knowledge of its dangerous channels, tides, currents, reefs and sandbanks, which made capture or reprisal virtually impossible. It was not until the end of the sixteenth century, when the cartographers began to map the remoter havens of the west coast more accurately, that time and the English navy caught up with her activities at sea.

There was another string to the O'Malleys' maritime bow. The employment of mercenaries was a common feature of

Gaelic warfare. The most renowned were the *galloglaigh* (foreign warriors), anglicised gallowglass who came from the isles and highlands of Scotland. They were hired annually, usually from May to October, by individual Gaelic chieftains or gaelicised Anglo-Norman lords, to fight their battles against an enemy chieftain or lord. The Clan Donnell was the gallowglass family most associated with the west of Ireland, and it was O'Malley ships which ferried them to and from their Scottish homeland. A branch of the Clan Donnell eventually settled permanently in Umhall, as sub-chieftains to the O'Malleys. If the gallowglass were the mercenaries of land, the O'Malleys could well be termed the mercenaries of the sea. O'Malley ships and crews were much sought after for hire by the warring chieftains and, to judge by the many references in the annals to O'Malley involvement in battles and skirmishes in Munster and Ulster, there was no scarcity of work. This mercenary tradition was continued by Granuaile and her sons until the early years of the seventeenth century.

The number and size of the ships in the O'Malley fleet have never been precisely determined. Irish-built trading vessels of the sixteenth century would have been a version of the clinker-built wooden cog of late medieval times. There are many references to the number of ships under the direction of individual members of the O'Malley clan. Tuathal O'Malley had seven ships under his command in Ulster in 1413, while in 1513 Eoghan O'Malley attacked Killybegs with three ships. Granuaile is recorded as commanding from three to twenty ships during the length of her career.

The 'galley' was the ship most associated with the O'Malleys and particularly Granuaile. Wooden-hulled and clinker-built, the galley had a shallow draught which allowed it to manoeuvre in low water. Powered by as many as thirty oars and a single sail, it was a speedy and versatile craft. The galley is thought to have evolved from the long ships — 'langskips' — of the Vikings, the intrepid seafarers from Scandinavia. The typical Viking ship had a keel, a mast of pine or ash measuring up to 11 metres, a square sail, a single row of oars on either side, and a side rudder affixed to the starboard quarter. It could attain a speed of up to ten knots.

Major developments in boatbuilding practices occurred particularly in the fifteenth century. The single-masted ship, difficult to steer and able to sail only with the wind, gave way to lateen-rigged two- and three-masted ships, such as the carrack, galleon, galleas and the galley. The Mediterranean type of galley had evolved from the ancient trireme but by the sixteenth century, its once three-tiered oar power had given way to a row of single oars on each side, manned by more than one rower. Long and narrow, these galleys often had as many as three masts, small decks fore and aft, and could accommodate as many as three hundred. Four of these galleys formed part of the Spanish Armada invasion of England in 1588, but they were ill-suited to the northern seas.

Experts appear reluctant to accept that the O'Malley galleys were more substantial craft than, for example, the smaller Hebridean galleys, commonly depicted on stone slabs and tombstone carvings. Descriptions of the galleys commanded by Granuaile in the sixteenth century show that they differ substantially in size from those of the Hebrides. Granuaile could offer Sidney in 1576 'three galleys and two hundred fighting men', capable of sailing anywhere in Ireland or in Scotland. The state papers further record in 1599:

> There are three very good galleys with Tibbott ne Long, son to Grany O'Malley . . . that will carry 300 men apiece. . . . There are no galleys in Ireland but these.[17]

In 1601 an English sea captain on patrol off the Mayo coast describes a skirmish with one of Granuaile's galleys, which was 'rowed with thirty oars and had on board ready to defend her 100 good shot'.[18] All the extant descriptions of Granuaile's galleys point to vessels of considerable size, perhaps a cross between the Hebridean galleys of the North and the galleys of the Mediterranean. What we know for certain is that they were of such strength, versatility and capability that for the space of fifty years they carried Granuaile and her army of 'two hundred fighting men', plus the plunder she accumulated en route, safely in most dangerous and unpredictable seas off the coasts of Ireland and Scotland.

Above: Contemporary English galley.

Left: Galley shown on 1590 Jobson map of Ulster.

Below: Granuaile's galley (author's impression, drawn by Jarlath Hayes)

In 1991 there was a re-enactment of the 400-mile voyage of Granuaile and Somerled, First Lord of the Isles, between Clew Bay and the Scottish isle of Stornoway. In the re-enactment, the replica galley had sixteen oars — just half the number recorded on the galleys of Granuaile. From descriptions in the state papers, it would appear that the galleys under Granuaile's command were not only substantial, but unique in Ireland. Colin Mudie designed the Brendan and Argo vessels for Tim Severin's epic voyages, as well as Granuaile's replica galley mentioned above. He cautions:

> We . . . have to look at historic craft not from any vantage point of technological superiority but from a much more humble station, appreciating how little we may know and how much we may be able to learn.

As a seafaring clan, part of whose income was derived from plunder and piracy, it was essential that O'Malley land bases were strategically situated — secure from retaliation as much as sheltered from the elements. The ring of O'Malley castles strung around the shoreline of Clew Bay fulfils these requirements admirably. The seat of the O'Malley chieftain was at Belclare castle (Dún Béal an Chláir — the Fort at the Mouth of the Plain, the plain of Murrisk). It was situated at the mouth of the Owenwee river on the site of an ancient *dún* or fort. Southeast inland from Belclare was a lake dwelling (*crannóg*) on the island in Moher lake, a place of refuge for the chieftain, his family and their valuables in time of danger. The family also possessed a castle at Cathair-na-Mart (Fort of the Beeves), situated alongside the present Westport House, a castle at Murrisk, Carrowmore, west of the town of Louisburgh, Kildawnet on Achill Island and the castle on Clare Island.

Clare Island and Achill are the only O'Malley castles extant. Although not the main residences of the O'Malley chieftain they afford some insight into the living conditions of a Gaelic clan from about the twelfth century. Both castles are strategically situated with commanding views of the sea, yet are undetectable by passing sea traffic. The castle on Clare Island is situated on a low rocky headland looking eastwards into the broad expanse of Clew Bay. It overlooks a fine crescent sandy beach,

Kildawnet Castle, Co. Mayo. An O'Malley residence (Commissioners of Public Works).

very suitable for beaching or mooring ships of shallow draught. Directly below it is a sheltered creek, having deep water at high tide. The castle is three stories high and once possessed battlements which gave an uninterrupted view of the open sea beyond the island. The three floor levels were connected by a stone stairway — straight rather than the spiral construction that was the more usual defensive access in this type of structure. The strong rectangular castle of Kildawnet is situated on a slight promontory on the west shore of Achill Sound. The Sound, with its strong and unpredictable currents, is a sea-passage connecting Clew Bay with Blacksod Bay to the north. With local knowledge it provided short and swift access or escape north or south between Achill Island and the mainland. The entrance to the Sound at the south end is protected by the island of Achill Beg. The castle itself is quite hidden from view from the outer sea and is surrounded by mountain and sea-scapes of the wildest splendour.

Like other Gaelic clans before the Reformation, the O'Malleys sustained orders of monks on their lands. The abbey at Murrisk was built by the O'Malleys in 1457 for the Augustinian friars, on land granted by the chieftain Thady O'Malley. It is beautifully situated on a quiet inlet of Clew Bay, beneath the towering peak of Croagh Patrick. Built in late Gothic style, its single-aisle church and a range of domestic buildings are now in semi-ruin. One of its best-preserved features is the delicate east window with its interlacing bar tracery and five trefoil parts. A striking feature of the abbey is its turreted south wall. At the west end of the church a partly vaulted tower once stood. Ironically, after the initial account of its foundation, nothing more was recorded about the abbey until notice of its proposed suppression on 27 March 1574, when Sir Peter Carew, in a despatch to the English lord deputy in Ireland, mentioned 'the abbey of Moyriske possessed by Friars or rebels so as her Majestie hath no commoditie in the same'.[19] In 1578 the Queen leased the lands of the abbey to James Garvey, but the friars were still in residence for some time longer, as in 1635 a chalice was presented to them inscribed: 'Pray for the souls of Theobald, Lord Viscount Mayo and his wife Maeve Ne Cnochoure who had me made for the monastery of Mureske

Murrisk Abbey, built by the O'Malleys. Drawing *c.* 1791 by Francis Grose (National Library of Ireland).

in the year of our lord 1635' (Theobald or Tibbot-ne-Long Bourke was the son of Granuaile). Murrisk Abbey would have featured largely in the lives of the O'Malley chieftains, being situated close to Belclare. It is possible that Granuaile was baptised and married there, and many of her ancestors and descendants lie buried beneath its now roofless walls.

The abbey on Clare Island was built by the O'Malleys two centuries before Murrisk, in 1224. Originally a Carmelite cell, it was later attached to the Cistercian house at Knockmoy. The later fifteenth-century church consisted of a nave, chancel and sacristy, as well as a range of domestic buildings to the north of the chapel which no longer exist. On the roof of the chancel can be seen one of the most unusual features of the abbey, thought, after recent and ongoing research and preservation work, to date from the fourteenth century. The paintings, which once covered the entire ceiling in a kaleidoscope of colour, depict mythical, human and animal figures, including dragons, a cockerel, stags, men on foot and on horseback, a harper, birds and trees. On the north wall of the chancel is a well-cut undated limestone slab showing a stallion salient on a wreath above a Norman-style helmet. It is thought to date from the early seventeenth century. A wild boar is trippant in the centre with three bows with arrows affixed pointing at it. At the right-hand base is a replica galley, with furled sail and five oars on a side, with the name 'O'Maille' and the motto *'Terra Mariq Potens'* in smaller lettering above. The entire shield and crest are surrounded by mantling. Beside the slab is a tomb canopy, with elegant cusped tracery, which tradition has always held to be the burial place of Granuaile, although recent research has suggested that it dates from the fourteenth century. The Norman-style helmet on the stone slab could possibly have relevance to Granuaile's second husband, Richard Bourke, the Mayo MacWilliam. The memorial and slab seem somewhat incongruous in such a remote and humble setting and, if tradition is to be believed, it is a fitting resting place for Granuaile.

After the initial setback at the hands of the De Burgos in the twelfth century, by which the jurisdiction of the O'Malley chieftains became restricted to Umhall Uachtarach and Achill, they continued their seafaring activities with renewed vigour. By the sixteenth century they were, as the English state papers acknowledge, 'much feared everywhere by sea'.[20] Politically they continued as an independent clan, the O'Malley chieftain being the only Gaelic chieftain in Mayo to retain his rank until the extinction of the title in the seventeenth century.

Opposite: Stone plaque showing O'Malley Arms, Clare Island Abbey.

2

The World of Granuaile

... men of sense
Hand down that Muireasc surely has its name,
From lovely Muirisc of the snowy hands,
The daughter of great Hugony the King,
She was a downright beauty, daring, bold,
And fixed her habitation near this bay,
Beneath the base of Cruachan Aigli, where
She ruled o'er hardy sailors and great men.[1]

The lines of this ancient poem eulogise a remote woman leader, called Muirisc, from whom the O'Malley Barony of Murrisk is said to have taken its name. Nothing more is known about her. But from the historical records it is obvious that in a prophetic way Muirisc's life presaged that of her sixteenth-century descendant, Granuaile, acknowledged leader also 'o'er hardy sailors and great men', over one thousand years later.

This connection between two women, from the same remote lordship, more than a millennium apart, is not as strange as it may appear. The warrior woman Muirisc lived in a time when Ireland was part of a Bronze-Age matriarchal culture in which the dominant deities were women. The name of Ireland itself is that of the mother-goddess Éirú or Éire, said to be one of the three legendary goddesses who ruled the country at the time of the invasion of the Milesians. The mystical Tuatha de Danaan, worshipped by the pagan Irish, had the all-powerful goddess Dana as their deity. In early Irish mythology, the sovereignty of Ireland (*Flaitheas Éireann*) was epitomised by a woman, invariably dressed in a blue cloak. Later still, in the

Celtic culture of the late Iron Age, which gave rise to the heroic legends of Fionn mac Cumhaill and the Fianna, and the Red Branch Knights of Ulster, the dominance of the woman warrior class was still very much in evidence. The prime hero of the Red Branch cycle, Cúchulainn, learned his battle prowess under the tutelage of the woman warrior Scathach. In combat he could overcome the warrior Princess Aoife only by resorting to trickery. Classical writers testified to the fighting skills of Celtic women. The Roman historian Tacitus confirmed that the Celts of Britain made no distinction as to sex in the choice of their military commanders, as in the case of Boadicea. The warrior Queen Maeve of Connaught was a powerful and fearless woman who was prepared to lead her army to war to achieve her ambition. Many of the warriors of the heroic legends of the Fenian and Ulster cycles used their mother's name in place of a patronymic, as the king of Ulster, Conor Mac (son of) Nessa, reinforcing the idea that in earlier times in Ireland descent was accomplished through the female line.

The demise in Ireland of a society ruled by powerful warrior women coincided with the advent of Christianity and the influence of Roman law which accompanied it. Roman society was male-dominated, the male having ultimate power over the lives of his dependent household, including women, as well as over his slaves. Descent was exclusively patrilineal, and inheritance strictly confined to the legitimate male heir. Christianity both inherited and defended this system. The writings of the early Christian saints such as Paul, John, Ambrose, Jerome and Augustine reflected the degraded position of women in Roman society. Augustine wrote of the 'horrible beastliness of women', that they were not born in God's image and should barely be tolerated on sufferance, let alone fill any position of authority. As Roman law and the Christian ethos began to dominate, this negative attitude towards women in society became enshrined in both state and religious laws and customs across Europe. By the sixteenth century, male historians and commentators, often clerical, perpetuated this attitude to women. However, amidst their reassertion of women's inferiority, weakness and unsuitability for high office, either in church or state, often lurked a fear which occasionally and inadvertently revealed man's acknowledgement of women's true potential. In his condemnation of their role in politics, in which he said that women were 'the cause of many troubles, have done great harm to those that govern cities, and have caused in them many divisions',[2] the sixteenth-century political analyst, Niccolo Machiavelli, for example, involuntarily acknowledges their ability.

The Romans overcame Celtic nations from Asia Minor right across to Britain. Only Ireland had remained outside Roman influence. Patrick brought Christianity to Ireland in the fifth century, and with it Roman law, which found itself in direct conflict with the indigenous law of Ireland, known as Brehon law. With Ireland's established tradition of a matriarchal culture, on no issue did both laws differ so fundamentally as on the status of women. Gradually, as Christianity infiltrated native Irish law, women's role in the power stakes in Ireland became diluted. Roman Salic law, which debarred women from power, became part of Brehon law. Gradually but insidiously the role of women was confined to childbearing, engaging in charitable deeds, for which they were occasionally lauded in the Irish annals, and being subservient to their husbands. In succeeding centuries in Ireland, while individual women — such as Gormflaith, Dervogilla, Margaret Fitzgerald, Countess of Ormond, Eleanor Butler, Countess of Desmond, Fionnuala Mac Donnell (*Iníon Dubh*) — managed to come to political prominence, it tended to be within the orbit of their husbands' or lovers' power struggles. By the time of Granuaile in the sixteenth century, an analogy for an independent woman ruler could be found only in myth and legend. This in turn caused the life of Granuaile herself to be relegated to myth rather than have to acknowledge that a woman could usurp what had come to be accepted as the exclusive role of man.

While Granuaile's career as a political leader by land can be said to mirror her Celtic woman ancestors, no such analogy can be found to explain her unique role as leader by sea. The sea and seafaring have from the beginning of time been considered a male preserve, and piracy one of the bastions of male domination. From the legendary odysseys of Jason,

Ulysses and Sinbad, to the exploratory voyages of Columbus, Da Gama and Magellan to the New Worlds, down to the time of Granuaile's more famous seafaring contemporaries, Frobisher, Drake and Raleigh, a woman's place was not aboard a ship, and most definitely not at the helm. Even in this age of 'equality', the sea and seafaring have in the main tended to remain a male preserve. Women commanders in the navies of the modern world are still a rarity. Women on ships were thought to be 'the devil's ballast', a bad omen, fated to bring storms and shipwreck. There was but place for one woman in the sailor's life at sea, and that was the sea goddess herself. From pagan Aphrodite to the Christian Mary Star of the Sea, the ocean goddess had to be placated, appeased and venerated to ensure a safe passage for those men who sailed on her heaving bosom. In Ireland, as elsewhere, seafaring was traditionally a male pursuit. Had Granuaile been born her father's son, she would probably not have achieved notoriety but would merely have been another O'Malley continuing the long-established seafaring tradition of his clan. The fact that as a woman she did just that makes her both unique and somehow incredible.

Granuaile was the only child of her parents, Owen 'Dubhdara' (Black Oak) O'Malley, chief of his name and ruler of Umhall Uachtarach, the Barony of Murrisk. His name conjures up the image of a strong, broad-shouldered, swarthy man, his shoulder-length hair cut in the customary 'glib' or fringe across his forehead. He dressed in tight worsted trews of the period, with a saffron *léine* or shirt, with wide sleeves, under a studded jack of tanned leather. A voluminous woollen cloak, deeply fringed around the neck, fastened with a gold pin, fell in folds around him. On his feet, square-toed brogues, and in the leather belt around his waist his *scian* or knife. A proud and independent chieftain, Dubhdara O'Malley was one of the few Gaelic chieftains of the time never to have submitted to the English crown.

Granuaile's mother was Margaret, daughter of Conchobhar Óg Mac Conchobhair, mic Maoilseachlain O'Malley, of the sept of Moher. According to contemporary English accounts, Gaelic women were

Gaelic chieftain and kerne (Derrick, 1581).

> Very comely creatures, tall, slender and upright. Of complexion very fayre and cleare skinned, but freckled, with tresses of bright yellow hayre, which they chayne up in curious knotts and devises. They are not strait laced nor plated in theyr youth, but suffered to grow at liberty so that you shall hardely see one crooked or deformed, but yet as the proverb is, soone ripe soone rotten. Theyre propensity to generation causeth that they cannot endure. They are women at thirteen and old wives at thirty. . . . Of nature they are very kind and tractable. . . .[3]

Whether Granuaile or her mother answered to this particular description of Gaelic women is unknown. As wife of a chieftain, Margaret O'Malley dressed in the traditional women's linen *léine*, reaching to the ankles, and over this a long tunic with a laced bodice, with perhaps a string of amber beads around her neck. Married women in Gaelic society tended to enfold their heads with a curious rolled linen headcloth. Margaret's duties would have centred on her husband's household, supervising the preparation of food, the upkeep of the castle and the entertainment of her husband's allies and guests.

Granuaile had a brother named Dónal, known as Dónal-na-Piopa (Dónal of the pipes) who was still living at the clan castle

The Gentlewoman of Ireland

The Civill Irish man

The Wilde Irish Woman

The Wilde Irish man

Sixteenth-century Gaelic men and women.

of Cathair-na-Mart in 1593. There is evidence to suggest that he was either illegitimate or Granuaile's half-brother by a woman other than her mother. In a bill of chancery, Granuaile's son was later to testify that she was 'the sole heir to the said Margrett',[4] her mother, and that she had inherited Margaret's lands in Umhall.

The earliest record of Granuaile's father, Dubhdara O'Malley, occurs in 1549, during the reign of Edward VI in England, in statutes compiled by the king's commissioners in Ireland. The statutes list the principal chieftains in the country. Among the Connaught chieftains is the name 'O'Mayle of Pomo'.[5] This is an interesting misnomer. The word *pomo* in Latin means apple. The Irish word *Umhall*, meaning territory, is pronounced similarly to the Irish word for apple, *úll*. Thus O'Malley of Umhall became O'Malley of Pomo in the papers.

Sixteenth-century Irishwoman.

The landscape of Ireland at the time of Granuaile's birth was virtually unchanged since the Anglo-Norman invasion of the twelfth century. The population is thought to have numbered no more than 700,000. Great primeval forests of oak, birch, ash, scots fir, hazel, willow, alder and holly, and dense woodlands covered a sizeable part of the countryside. There were large tracts of marsh and bog-lands interspersed by arable and open pasturelands. There were few roads and even fewer bridges. Most of the towns were situated on the coast or on the navigable rivers. Because of the absence of roads and bridges, travel was extremely difficult and there was much recourse to travel by water, both by river and sea. The mountain pass, the forest pathway and the river ford were the all-important keys to communication, and their control was often the source of warfare. Behind a natural screen of forest, water and mountain, the Gaelic world flourished. There were no accurate maps of the country, and the English kings who claimed lordship over Ireland knew as little about the country as they did about the far-off Americas. The actual mapping of Ireland towards the end of the sixteenth century was a major contributory factor to the eventual submission of the Gaelic world at the beginning of the seventeenth century. The maps were in themselves symbols of the extension of English control.

Granuaile was born at the beginning of an era which was to prove a milestone in the history of Ireland. The effects of the Anglo-Norman invasion of the twelfth century were by then scarcely evident. English power was confined to Dublin and the Pale, a small area stretching north, south and west of the city. The native Irish held all Ulster, with the exception of parts of Down and Antrim, most of Connaught, the north and west of Munster, the midlands and west Leinster. The native customs, laws and language, which had received a reversal at the time of the invasion, flourished again. Even the descendants of the Anglo-Norman dynasties, like the earls of Kildare, Desmond and Ormond, and the De Burgos of Connaught, had become gaelicised, becoming 'more Irish than the Irish themselves' to varying degrees, depending on their political and geographical proximity to Dublin.

At the time of Granuaile's birth, Ireland was divided into as many as

> sixty counties . . . where reigneth sixty chief captains . . . that liveth only by the sword and obeyeth to no other temporal person but only to himself that is strong. And every of the said captains maketh war and peace for himself and holdeth by the sword and hath imperial jurisdiction within his room and obeyeth to no other person, English or Irish, except only to such persons as may subdue him by the sword.[6]

Ireland was not like England, where the Tudors, starting with

Henry VII a few decades previously, had succeeded in bringing the powerful feudal magnates to heel, claiming a divine right to rule over them. No such central figure of authority had emerged from the whirlpool of disunity in Ireland to mould the regained power of the chieftains and gaelicised Anglo-Norman lords into a viable centralised government. Instead, inter-clan warfare, which was to be the Achilles heel of Gaelic resistance later in the century, was endemic.

Granuaile's father, as one of the 'sixty chief captains' referred to, ruled the lordship of Umhall according to Brehon law. The Gaelic legal system was distinct to Ireland and had evolved over the centuries from its Celtic origins, absorbing some aspects of the two main outside incursions — Christianity in the fifth century and the Anglo-Norman invasion with its feudal laws in the twelfth century. The very nature of Gaelic society and its capacity to assimilate foreign influences, had made it resilient. Gaelic society comprised clans or extended family groupings of independent chieftaincies. The chieftain was elected by members of the ruling sept or family within the clan and did not inherit by feudal primogeniture. By Gaelic law a brother could succeed a brother, a nephew an uncle, or a younger son a father, to the chieftaincy. A custom known as 'tanistry' had been introduced whereby the elected successor (*tánaiste*) to the chieftain was chosen during the chieftain's lifetime. The Salic law, which prohibited women from being eligible for election, was, by the sixteenth century, long part of the system. The tenure of land also differed from the feudal system and was conducted according to a complex method of land distribution, differing from region to region, whereby on the death of a chieftain or a co-heir, or in some areas on an annual basis each May Day, the clan lands were redistributed among the ruling or landholding members of the clan. The chieftain enjoyed a life interest only in the lands pertaining to the chieftaincy. The fosterage of the sons of an overlord with a sub-lord was a common practice and further strengthened the links of dependency between them. Sons born outside wedlock were not discriminated against either socially or legally. They were eligible for election to the chieftaincy and enjoyed the same inheritance rights as sons born within wedlock.

Principal Lordships, sixteenth-century Ireland.

The chieftain's power was based on a system of clientship (*célsine*) whereby he strove to have as many *úir-rí* (sub-lords) under his control as possible. In lieu of his protection, his sub-lords were forced to pay him onerous dues and tributes, such as a specific annual payment of cattle, sheep, grain, flour, honey or candles, to the provision of lodging and entertainment, known as cuddy (*cuid oíche*), for the chieftain and his retinue. They were also obliged to fulfil specific duties, including the provision of a 'rising out', an agreed number of armed men to assist the overlord in war, just as the O'Malley chieftain provided for his overlord, the MacWilliam Bourke. Likewise, the O'Malley chieftain received from his sublords in Umhall, the MacGibbons and the Clandonnells, 'the chief rents of barley, butter and money as well as all fines for bloodshed, all skins of animals killed or to be killed . . . with all customs and other casualties.'[7]

Debarred from the chieftaincy and therefore from power, Gaelic woman, as the annals confirm, rarely were acknowledged other than as wives of chieftains, doers of charitable works, donors of bequests to abbeys and monasteries, and occasionally as patrons of educational establishments. Politically some featured in the background as disruptive or negative influences in the politics being pursued by their husbands or lovers — the infamous Dervogilla O'Rourke, for example. Some, like Eleanor Butler FitzGerald, Countess of Desmond, and Margaret FitzGerald Butler, Countess of Ormond, filled the vacuum caused by their husband's political inadequacies but received little official acknowledgement in the process. While Gaelic law mitigated against women in the political sense, in other respects, particularly in the area of marriage and divorce, it accorded them much more protection and many more rights than their European counterparts. It allowed them the right to retain their maiden names throughout their marriage(s). It also permitted women, like Granuaile and her mother before her, to own and administer their own land and property, a practice which contrasted sharply with English law where a husband enjoyed absolute control over his wife's possessions. In a late sixteenth-century poem composed in honour of Granuaile's son, Tibot-ne-Long (Tibóid na Long) Bourke, it is notable that he is referred to as 'the ruddy-cheeked heir of Grainne',[8] his mother, rather than his father, a further indication that Granuaile was a proprietor in her own right.

Sixteenth-century warfare (Derrick, 1581).

Together with the ruling class, Gaelic society was composed also of freemen and landless labourers, referred to alternatively as betagh (*biatach*) or churls. The betagh were the backbone of Gaelic society. They worked from dawn to dusk for their chieftain and received few privileges in return. There was also the learned class (*aes dána*), which included the poets (*filí*), the most revered of all classes, the bards and the dispensers of law, the brehons (*breitheamh*) or judges. There were two classes of military men, the gallowglass and the kerne (*ceithearn*). The gallowglass were, as previously mentioned, mercenary soldiers from the Scottish isles and highlands. Of great strength and stature, they dressed from neck to heel in chain mail and conical iron helmets, and were armed with great swords and the infamous battleaxe. The kerne were the light infantry of the chieftain's army. Armed with bows and arrows, javelins and darts, their speed and agility were of special importance on marshy land where they could outrun and outmanoeuvre even enemy horsemen. Gaelic forces seldom fought in military formation. They attacked by making rapid and irregular forays, then withdrawing, using their knowledge of the terrain, of woodland, forest, marsh and bog, to their tactical advantage. Prior to the Elizabethan conquest of the country, inter-clan rivalry, disputes over succession to the chieftaincy and cattle raiding were the principal causes of the almost incessant inter-clan warfare.

Despite the Reformation in England, Ireland still adhered to the old religion. Gaelic Catholicism, however, differed greatly from that of the Roman Church. The sweeping reforms of previous centuries had, by and large, failed to make much impression on its structure and ethos, and the Gaelic church adhered to many practices of its Celtic pagan roots. A chieftain's coronation ceremony was not conducted in a church but at the pagan rath of his remote ancestors. A pattern of hereditary clergy had evolved where members of a particular family, often non-clerical, were invested with abbacies and bishoprics. Some of the clergy, including bishops and abbots, were either married or maintained concubines. Many of the aristocratic families sought and were given licence to marry within the prohibited degrees of consanguinity. A form of Celtic secular marriage prevailed. Trial marriages were common and divorce was long established as a legal right. The sacraments were celebrated haphazardly and many of the clergy were illiterate.

The living conditions of Gaelic chieftains were geared to the predominantly agrarian and military lifestyle they pursued, a feature reflected in the construction of their dwellings, which were built primarily for shelter and defence, rather than for comfort. Before the advent of cannon, such structures were virtually impossible to capture. Dubhdara O'Malley lived in the stone fortress of Belclare, a somewhat larger edition of the castles of Clare Island and Kildawnet. These castles or towers were four or five stories high with a bawn, enclosed by high walls, often with a small barbican protecting the entrance. The castle was lit by narrow slit windows, called loops, and had turrets and crenellations below the roof, usually made of thatch, occasionally of lead. The castle was dark and damp inside, especially the lower floors, which were used mainly for storage. The chieftain and his family lived in the upper apartments, which were brighter and often had a fireplace. The walls were whitewashed and hung with antlers, skins and green-leafed branches. The furniture was minimal and basic — wooden tables, benches, cupboards and bedsteads. Around the outskirts of the castle nestled the beehive dwellings of the chieftain's followers.

While remains of the stone fortresses of the chieftains dot the Irish landscape, few, if any, examples of the dwellings of the landless majority have survived. Writing at the turn of this century, a visitor to Achill Island saw one of the last surviving examples of these ancient dwellings, and described it thus:

> a low circular room, thatched outside but within ceiled with stout rafters, a massive bog pine pillar in the centre holds up the roof. There is a low door, no window and a small hole in the roof to let out the smoke . . . one or two little sleeping berths close to the fire, a stone ledge for a candle end, a bag of meal within reach for the stirabout and an iron pot which cooks food for man and beast. . . . The stone walls of the building are several feet thick.[9]

Accounts of the lifestyle of sixteenth-century Gaelic Irish chieftains were recorded mainly by English military commanders during the turbulent decades of the second half of the century. Their portrayal of the customs of the country and people they were sent to conquer, which differed from those pertaining to England, is not surprisingly unflattering and biased. Some non-military English travellers, however, were somewhat more objective in their observations. Recording a visit to a chieftain's castle, one wrote:

> The lady of the house meets you with her train. . . . Salutations past, you shall be presented with all the drinks in the house, first the ordinary beer, then aquavitae, then sack, then old ale . . . The fire is prepared in the middle of the hall. . . . The table is spread and plentifully furnished with [a] variety of meats, but ill cooked and without sauce. . . . They feast together with great jollity and healths around. . . . The harper begins to tune and singeth Irish rhymes of ancient making.[10]

The main meal of the day was taken in the evening. For the landless majority, a porridge made of oatmeal and milk, flavoured with butter or honey, and oaten griddle cakes, was the staple diet. For the noble classes, food was plentiful and varied. Beef, mutton, venison, poultry and game were widely consumed with vegetables such as cabbage, onions, wild garlic, watercress and leeks. Salmon, herring and shellfish were an added luxury to the diet of those with access to rivers and the sea. Dillisk, eaten with butter, was considered a delicacy. Meat was generally boiled or roasted on a spit (*bir*). Buttermilk was a favourite drink of all classes and was 'wonderfully cold and pleasing',[11] according to one English description. Native *uisce beatha* or whiskey, ale and great quantities of wine from France and Spain were widely consumed. Mead, a honey-based drink, was considered a special beverage, and the area that produced it praiseworthy. O'Malley's territory of Umhall, particularly in the vicinity of Murrisk, was notable for mead, as the old laudatory expression, 'mead-abounding Murrisk' acknowledges. Meals were served in the chieftain's house on low wooden trestle tables. Meat was placed on large wooden or pewter platters from which everyone helped themselves by cutting slivers with a knife. Food was eaten with knife and hands; forks were still a rarity.

In summer, like their contemporaries, Dubhdara O'Malley and his household left Belclare to go 'booleying', to graze the clan cattle herds in the mountain uplands, where they lived in temporary accommodation. This custom had its origins in Celtic times and survived in O'Malley territory until recently when,

> grazing in common was lately found by the Congested Districts Board, in full operation on Clare Island and in re-arranging the land there they wisely left the old custom undisturbed.[12]

In the seventeenth century, an English traveller, John Dunton, while on a visit to Granuaile's grandson, Murrough-na-Mart O'Flaherty, a chieftain in Connemara, described living conditions during a booley:

> The house was one entire long roome without any partition. In the middle of it was the fireplace with a large wood fire which was no way unpleasing tho in summer time. It had no chimney but a vent hole for the smoake at the ridge.

Chieftain feasting (Derrick, 1581).

He was told by the O'Flaherty chieftain

> That they had newly put up this for a 'booley' or summer habi-
> tation, the proper dwelling or mansion house being some
> miles farther neare the sea, and such a one they commonly
> built everie yeare in some one place or other, and thatched it
> with rushes. I had sheets and soft white blankets . . . and they
> assur'd me no man ever gott cold lyeing on the green rushes,
> which indeed are sweet and cleane, being changed everie day
> if rain hinders not.

Dunton was entertained by O'Flaherty during his stay:

> We had at dinner no less than a whole beef boyl'd and roasted,
> and what mutton I know not so profewsly did they lay it on the
> table. At the end where the lady sate was placed an heap of
> oaten cakes above a foot high, such another in the middle and
> the like at the lower end, at each side of the middle heap were
> placed two large vessels filled with Troandor or the whey with
> buttermilk and sweet milk. . . . We had such ale . . . and bul-
> caan, and after dinner myn host ordered his doggs to be gotten
> ready to hunt the stagg. He had his horse sadled and one for
> me too. . . . Eighteen long greyhounds and above thirty foote-
> men made up the company.[13]

Such a lifestyle was redolent of the ancient sagas of the Celtic
world from whence it derived.

Cattle were the principal source of wealth of the Gaelic
clans, and cattle hides a major export. Fishing was the main
source of income for the O'Malleys, and the building and maintenance of the clan's fleet of fishing and trading vessels, nets
and other fishing equipment were an essential part of clan
work. Leisure time was spent hunting the red deer which
abounded in the Umhalls, and also the ferocious wild boar,
which was the emblem on the O'Malley shield. Falconry was
another favourite activity of the Gaelic chieftains and the best
falconries were to be found in west Connaught. Travelling
storytellers and musicians entertained the chieftain's household during the winter months. These itinerant entertainers
were also an essential source of news and gossip. Chess, dice
and card-playing were popular pastimes, and professional
gamblers known as 'carrows' (*gearbhach*) toured the country-

side and were eagerly received in the houses of the chieftains and lords.

Such was the state of Ireland at the time of Granuaile's birth, circa 1530. The prevailing ethos, language, laws, customs and dress were Gaelic. The power of the Gaelic chieftains and gaelicised Anglo-Norman lords was at its highest. England's authority had long ceased to have effect on the daily lives of the majority of the people, with the exception of those in Dublin and the Pale. Yet the reversal of English dominance had not been translated into political power by the Gaelic chieftains. For the greater part of the century, Ireland remained devoid of any unifying ideological stimulus. A state of disunity and fragmented loyalties prevailed, and energy and intellect were wasted on petty power struggles. In sixteenth-century Ireland, tribal warfare, cattle-raiding and blood money were as much part of daily life as they had been in the time of Queen Maeve and Cúchulainn. This situation contrasted sharply with most of Europe and more lately with Ireland's nearest neighbour, England, where the yearning for change, discovery, knowledge and the achievements of the Renaissance and Reformation permeated and animated, and where one centralised authority demanded the allegiance of all.

Such was the antique society that bore and bred Granuaile, a society which, unless it adapted to the fundamental changes of the world outside its own orbit, was destined to perish. Like her era, Granuaile, in her role as a woman warrior leader, was a product of the past, and unless she could adapt, she too would have to pay the price of inflexibility.

3

Fortuna Favet Fortibus
(O'Flaherty Clan Motto)

As with Gaelic children generally, Granuaile's childhood is undocumented. From the meagre information relating to children in the sixteenth century we know that the period of childhood was short-lived. In Ireland the custom of fosterage dictated that the sons of the aristocracy left the home of their natural parents as early as six years old. Since succession to the chieftaincy was by the selection of the fittest, their education centred, like that of their Celtic forebears, on mastering the skills and techniques of warfare, the use of weaponry, riding stirrupless on horseback and proving their mettle as potential chieftains by raiding their neighbours. Such concentration on physical prowess might well have been at the expense of learning. Judging by the crosses made in lieu of signatures on many official state documents of the period, it is clear that many chieftains were illiterate. This fact, however, must be counterbalanced by the existence of scribes, lawyers and *filí* in the households of most of the prominent chieftains of the time. The function of these people was to provide the chieftain with the necessary written and verbal skills and advice for the administration of his lordship.

While knowledge of the rearing and education of boys in sixteenth-century Gaelic Ireland is vague, information on the rearing of the daughters of the aristocracy is virtually non-existent. As in the case of political power, women's access to the bardic ranks was no longer permitted. The days of the female bard and poetess, of the fabled Liadán and Feidelm, were no more. Like the chieftaincy, the honoured ranks of the *filí* were confined to men. The all-male-administered bardic, monastic, and secular post-Norman schools had no place for female pupils. The scanty records of the few nunneries established in Ireland provide no evidence of any great female scholarship. Yet some Gaelic women — usually the daughters, wives or concubines of the learned classes — managed, despite the education bias and oftentimes denunciations of their male counterparts, to circumvent the system and become more learned than their menfolk. In the letters of such contemporary Irish noblewomen as Eleanor Butler, Countess of Desmond and Joan Butler, Countess of Ormond, the handwriting, extensive vocabulary and well-turned phrases display a shrewd and consummate knowledge of the political arena. This, combined with their ability to negotiate skilfully with the most prominent and astute political minds of the time, is testimony to some degree of a formal education. In terms of such political acumen and negotiating skill, it is clear from her correspondence that Granuaile was on par with her Anglo-Norman sisters. Her extant correspondence, numbering some five petitions to Queen Elizabeth and the Lord Treasurer, Lord Burghley, and her fascinating autobiographical answers in 1593 to the Lord Treasurer's set of eighteen questions, reveals an equally shrewd and knowledgeable mind. From the penmanship of her correspondence, however, it seems unlikely that Granuaile was the actual scribe, but from the evasiveness and political cunning displayed therein, she was undoubtedly the author.

Education in Ireland during the sixteenth century was dispensed in a somewhat haphazard way, confined, as in most European countries, to the religious, aristocratic and merchant classes. The Renaissance influence and the aspirations of the Christian Humanists, such as Erasmus and Thomas More, towards making education available to all levels of the laity, and particularly their commitment to the education of women, scarcely touched Ireland. Where it did, it was confined to the lordships of the Anglo-Normal magnates, the cities and the Pale. The wives of the Gaelic chieftains in the main immersed themselves in rearing their families and managing their households.

By the mid-1500s, Ireland had long abandoned her claim to be the 'island of saints and scholars'. The great monastic schools of Ireland's golden era, which had attracted scholars from all over Europe, were no more. Unlike other European countries, there was no university. A few religious schools, mainly teaching canon law and Latin, were still in existence. The sixteenth century was not a golden era of letters in Ireland. The poet's craft was mainly expended on eulogising and elegising Gaelic chieftains and Anglo-Norman lords. But some schools were maintained by the *filí*, where the intricate metres of Gaelic verse were taught to members of the hereditary bardic families. Much of the bardic teaching was verbally rather than literally transmitted, as were the legal tenets handed down by the brehons. As well as verse-making the bardic schools taught Latin, which would seem to have been understood and used by clergy and laity alike, a knowledge of the Greek and Roman classics, philosophy, some mathematics and probably reading and writing in Gaelic and Latin. The pupils were mainly those sons of the Gaelic aristocracy who had neither the means nor the desire to seek education in the universities of England or the Continent.

The evidence that Granuaile received some formal schooling is confined to the extant documentation relating to her petitions and answers and to the fact that she is traditionally credited with conversing in Latin in her audience in 1593 with the erudite English queen, Elizabeth I. However, that she may also have been conversant in English is likely, as referenced by her meeting and conversation in 1577 with the famous poet-courtier, Sir Philip Sidney. The source of Granuaile's education was perhaps the two houses of friars maintained by her father at Murrisk and on Clare Island.

But given the wholly unorthodox role she was later to adopt, contrary both to law and social convention, and to her undoubted ability and success as an active leader for over forty years, it is more likely that the brunt of Granuaile's education was geared, where her interest lay, in her father's world of ships, trade, politics and power. To achieve even part of what she was accused of by the English administration in Ireland, she had to be accomplished in the skills of seafaring. Her ability to sail her ships to Scotland, England, and quite possibly to Spain and Portugal, ranks her among the best of sixteenth-century mariners. Doubly endowed with O'Malley blood from both her parents, seafaring came naturally to her. This aptitude and affinity with the sea, her clan's benefactor in war and in peace, undoubtedly shaped her character and outlook. It is reasonable to assume that she accompanied her father as a young girl on many of his fishing and trading voyages, and from him learned about seafaring. And there was much to learn: the tides and currents, the moods of the sea, to become, as O'Dugan wrote, 'a prophet of the weather' like her ancestors, to know when to set sail and when to stay ashore, to know the ability of the ships she sailed, about canvas and hawser, ballast and anchor, to navigate by star and by compass, to learn about the perils of the treacherous Irish coastline, the protruding rocky headlands and hidden reefs. The later threats of English warships out to capture her, or competitors in the piracy trade out to relieve her of her cargo and her life, augmented the hazards. Judging by the success and duration of her career by sea, Dubhdara O'Malley surely taught his daughter well. It was perhaps her father's character, authority and even his physical attributes that drew Granuaile to emulate him in later life, to dress like him, to adopt his lifestyle and, in effect, to become more like a son than a daughter.

Her choice of career, notwithstanding her family tradition, was unique for a woman. The sea and seafaring were and have ever tended to be the exclusive domain of men. The nature of the environment, both from a physical and a decorum point of view, tended to exclude women. Male moral values pervaded ship life. Swearing, disregard for hygiene, carousing and violence, as well as the sexual difficulty posed by the presence of a female among an all-male crew, made seafaring an unattractive and dangerous option for a woman. Seafaring in the sixteenth century was not for the fainthearted. Conditions aboard ship were primitive, privacy non-existent. For a woman's physique it must have been intolerable — skin toughened under the barrage of wind and spray, hands hardened and nails split by hawser and canvas, bare feet chafed from the roughly hewn swaying boards, sodden woollen trews and linen shirts clinging uncomfortably, unappetising food lodged undigested, the discharge of natural bodily functions lacking the usual privacy. To give birth on a bucking galley on the high seas, as Granuaile later did, seems unimaginable. Life aboard ship, on a voyage of trade or fishing, could often be boring, with little but singing and gaming to help relieve the tedium of long days and nights at sea.

Piracy and plundering by sea were practised by Granuaile as by her ancestors. In remote coastal areas, far from the watchful eye of government, piracy tended to flourish. In the sixteenth century, the west coast of Ireland was still far enough removed from English authority, as the pirate havens of the West Indies were to be a century later. Piracy in any climate was a grim and dangerous occupation, the penalty for which was death by hanging. Many of Granuaile's English contemporaries were 'seen off at Wapping Old Stairs', the execution site on the Thames. Those in the West Indies who dared to go 'on the account' often breathed their last at Gallows Point, east of the old pirate city of Port Royal in Jamaica. Two of the more notorious female pirates who followed in Granuaile's wake over a century later, Ann Bonny and Mary Read, 'pleaded their bellies' at their trial in Jamaica to escape the hangman's noose. To be a woman in command of pirate galleys, as Granuaile was for the space of forty years, demanded a stern but fair hand to keep her crew in control, and success at her trade of 'maintenance'. To fulfil the basic requirement of piracy, 'no prey, no pay', she also had to oversee the fair sharing out of plunder and, above all, she needed to be more daring and courageous than any of her men.

There has always been much speculation as to how Grace O'Malley became known, mainly through folklore, as Granuaile (Gráinne Mhaol, the word 'maol' meaning bald). It is likely that the name Granuaile is a corrupt amalgam of the Gaelic Gráinne Uí Mháille or alternatively Gráinne Umhaill (Grace of Umhall). There are many anglicised versions of her name contained in the English state papers, including Grany O'Maly, Grany Imallye, Granny Nye Male, Grany O' Mayle, Granie ny Maille, Granny ni Maille, Grany O'Mally, Grayn ny Mayle, Grane ne Male, Grainy O'Maly and Granee O'Maillie.

Granuaile spent her childhood at the family residences of Belclare and Clare Island. There was little to disturb the traditional way of life pursued by her family. The seasons and the sea dictated the ebb and flow of life in the O'Malley household as they had done for their ancestors: fishing and trading voyages, storms, occasional shipwrecks — welcomed, as in all coastal communities as rewards from the sea — summer booleying and deer hunting, the yearly courtesy visit to and by O'Malley's overlord MacWilliam, the excitement at the arrival of strolling musicians and mummers and particularly the carrows, were the annual highlights. To judge by contemporary reports, the Gaelic chieftains seemed addicted to the carrows who, according to one observer, 'so infected the public meetings of the people and the private houses of the lords. . . .'[1]

Grace clearly became as 'infected' as her peers, and her gambling skills were later commemorated in a sixteenth-century poem addressed to the Ulster chieftain Shane O'Doherty:

> *Gráinne na gcearbhach do creach*
> Grace of the gamblers he plundered[2]

This way of life, followed by her clan for centuries, was, however, about to face its ultimate challenge. Remote from Dublin, the centre of English power in Ireland, hidden behind a protective screen of wood, forest, bog and the river Shannon, the O'Malleys, like most western clans, were little concerned with the schemes and plots being hatched far away by an English king. These plots would be carried to a decisive and bloody conclusion by a daughter the king had once spurned but who was destined to become England's greatest monarch and Ireland's most determined conqueror.

The winds of change in Ireland's relationship with her powerful neighbour, England, began to blow more fiercely towards the last decade of the reign of England's turbulent monarch, Henry VIII. From 1529 to 1536, the Reformation and his matrimonial problems commanded Henry's attention. The revolt and ruthless extinction of the House of Kildare in 1537 directed the king's gaze across the Irish Sea to his neglected lordship. Rather than resort to costly warfare, Henry instituted a policy of 'surrender and regrant', in an attempt to gain control in Ireland. To implement this policy, Henry had himself confirmed 'King of Ireland' instead of 'Lord of Ireland', the title held by previous English monarchs. Thus began the new 'Kingdom of Ireland', which was to last until 1800.

The surrender and regrant policy was based on the theory that all lands held by the Gaelic and Anglo-Norman lords depended on the crown of England. On submission to the king, the chieftain or lord would receive back his lands, in the king's name, provided that he agreed to rule by English law and attend the king's parliament in Dublin. In return, he would receive an English title suited to his rank. Throughout 1541 some of the most prominent chieftains and lords submitted to the king's deputy in Dublin. Murrough, chieftain of the great O'Brien clan in Munster, was created Earl of Thomond. In Ulster, the O'Neill, regarded by many as the hereditary king of Ireland, submitted and accepted the title Earl of Tyrone. In Connaught, Ulick Burke, the Upper MacWilliam of Galway, was created Earl of Clanrickard.

Thus began the subtly effective Tudor conquest of Ireland. As the chieftains and lords accepted the terms and titles of the English king, so they were bound to abandon the Brehon laws and customs that had endowed them with their position of power in the first place. Their acceptance of the terms ran contrary to the Gaelic principles of election and land tenure. Some chieftains felt coerced into acceptance; others accepted readily out of greed or disillusionment with the impermanence of the Gaelic system which allowed for little continuity; but most accepted only for as long as it suited their own purpose. It was a triumph for Henry VIII who, at his death in 1547, had, through a relatively peaceful and inexpensive yet effective policy, extended his authority, nominally at least, over Leinster and parts of Ulster, Munster and Connaught. In the remainder of the country, suppression of the native laws and customs would take longer, but the machinery for their decline had been firmly set in motion.

As yet, Mayo remained untouched by the changes. Up to

now the affairs of the country, even of Connaught, were of little consequence to the O'Malley chieftain or his immediate neighbours, provided that they were allowed to rule their territories unhindered by either Irish or English. In Umhall, the fishing was good and O'Malley could afford to thumb his nose at the avaricious merchants of Galway, and choose his own markets. The only blip on the scene may have been that his daughter looked set to become the sailor her half-brother Dónal never was, and in the male-oriented society of Gaelic Ireland that was something hardly to be countenanced by any father. There was little future for a woman inclined towards male pursuits. The only career move for a woman was towards the marriage bed, and for the daughter of a chieftain, marriage must also pay political dividends.

Grace was about sixteen years old when she was married to Dónal O'Flaherty, son of Gilledubh O'Flaherty, chieftain of the Ballinahinch sept, the senior ruling branch of the extensive clan. The O'Flahertys were rulers of the vast, rugged territory of Iar Chonnacht, roughly equivalent to modern-day Connemara. They were a warlike clan, as their motto, 'fortune favours the bold', implies. Yet unlike most Gaelic clans of the period, for decades O'Flahertys had co-existed in relative harmony with their neighbours, the O'Malleys, and were allies in war. For Dubhdara O'Malley, politically the match between his daughter and the O'Flaherty chieftain was a satisfactory one. By Gaelic custom, Dónal was the elected *tánaiste* to the chieftain of all the O'Flaherty septs, and one day would be ruler of all Iar Chonnacht. At his marriage to Granuaile, he was chieftain of the Barony of Ballinahinch. His chief castle was on the coast at Bunowen, some two miles south of Slyne Head, the most westerly point in Connaught. It had a deep harbour with good anchorage and was sheltered from the west by the Hill of Doon. Granuaile's new home was separated from Umhall by the deep fjord of Killary and by some of the most spectacular scenery in the country. It was bounded to the north west by the Twelve Bens; in the distance southeastwards were the extensive island-strewn waters of Lough Corrib; while all around lay the stones, moors and lakelets of Connemara.

As the daughter of a chieftain, Granuaile did not go empty-handed to her marriage. As was customary in the sixteenth century she brought a substantial dowry (*spréidh*) to her husband in the form of cattle, horses, sheep and household goods. Special 'sureties for the restitution of the same', according to Granuaile's own testimony 'in manner and in form as she hath delivered it', were an integral and important part of the matrimonial contract, in case of the death of her husband or, as she testified, 'at other times they were divorced.'[3] Since divorce was quite prevalent among the Gaelic aristocracy, the marriage contracts made provisions for that eventuality. On the death of her husband or upon divorce, the wife was entitled to receive in full the dowry she had brought with her to the marriage. In some parts of Gaelic Ireland a special tax or imposition (*cáin beag*) was raised within the lordship for the maintenance of the chieftain's wife. On the death of the chieftain, the widow did not normally receive any part of his property; as Granuaile later stated, 'the countries of Connaught among the Irishry never yeiled any thirds to any woman surviving the chieftain',[4] which made the imposition of sureties for the restitution of a woman's dowry a vital part of the marriage contract.

Like most young brides, Granuaile could well be expected to experience a sense of isolation and homesickness in her new surroundings. The role expected of her now was that of wife, homemaker and potential mother — a role at variance with the independent seafaring career she had sought. To be at the command of her husband, submissive to him in all things, must surely have been anathema to Granuaile. Her upbringing had been in an environment of equality — the sea made no distinction between female and male sailors. By the later evidence of her relationship with her second husband, it is difficult to imagine her remaining long in the role of dutiful wife. Her young husband, as his sobriquet Dónal-an-Chogaidh (Dónal of the Battles) suggests, was a reckless and truculent chieftain — hardly a man who would allow his role to be usurped by a wife. A clash of personalities seemed inevitable. But whether contrary to her wishes or not, for a time at least, Granuaile fulfilled what society, her father and her husband deemed to be her role. She bore two sons, Owen and Murrough, and a daughter, Margaret, perhaps named after her own mother, of whom nothing has been recorded but her name and ancestry and the fact that she inherited land in her own right in Umhall.

However marriage may have altered Granuaile's way of life, there was little change evident in that of her husband. In 1549 Dónal was implicated in the murder of Walter Fada (Tall) Bourke, son of David Bourke, the *tánaiste* to the MacWilliam of Mayo. The murder was committed at the O'Flaherty castle of Invernan in Moycullen, west of Galway city. It is recorded that Dónal murdered Walter at the instigation of his sister, Finola, stepmother of Walter, so that her own son, Richard, might be the sole heir of his father and a step closer to becoming the MacWilliam. Dónal's likely gain from the murder is less clear. A possible incentive might have been the promise of an alliance between himself and Richard, when, as the O'Flaherty and the MacWilliam respectively, together they would control Mayo and Iar Chonnacht. However, only part of the plot was realised, while the rest turned out in a way that neither Dónal nor Finola, and, least of all, Granuaile could have anticipated.

While her husband continued to play the role of warlord, constantly feuding with his neighbours, particularly the Joyce clan with whom he was in dispute over possession of a castle on Lough Corrib, Granuaile was not content to be a stay-at-home wife. Judging by later records which accuse her of being in action for over forty years, it is clear that what Gaelic law denied her as a woman she simply took for herself. Tradition also holds that during her marriage to Dónal-an-Chogaidh, whether through his inadequacies as a chieftain or simply by her own inclination, Granuaile superseded him in his authority over his clan and, more incredibly still, was accepted by his clansmen to such a degree that many of them later chose to leave Iar Chonnacht with her.

Bunowen Castle was an ideal base from which to launch a new chapter in her seafaring activities. Around this time the first reports of her attacks on ships sailing into the busy port of Galway were recorded. Galway city was hostile to the O'Flahertys, about whom the Galway citizens had inscribed over the west gate of the city 'From the ferocious O'Flahertys, Good Lord deliver Us'. Because the corporation of the city imposed taxes on the clans who traded there, Grace and her followers doubtless sought to do the same on the seas off their territory. Out of the cover of the coastal islands and bays their galleys swooped on the lumbering merchantmen. Negotiations for safe passage into Galway were rewarded by a toll or part of the cargo. Laden with the agreed or extracted spoil, Granuaile and her men disappeared into some uncharted bay on the indented coastline. The corporation of Galway city was power-less against such attacks and conveyed its frustration to the English Council in Dublin:

> The continuing roads used by the O'Malleys and O'Flaherties with their galleys along our coasts, where there have been taken sundry ships and barks bound for this poor town, which they have not only rifled to the utter overthrow of the owners and merchants, but also have most wickedly murdered divers of young men to the great terror of such as would willingly traffic. . . .[5]

Whether leadership was forced upon Granuaile out of neces-sity or otherwise, there had to be a receptive ambitious need within her which drove her to take the mantle of power at a time when society sought to consign women to a life of do-mesticity and dependence. Gaelic society demanded that its leaders were strong of will and body, able to protect those who gave them allegiance and to defend their domain. Any sign of weakness or frailty on the part of a chieftain was certain to unleash the ambitions of competitors for his office. To retain control of her wild crewmen, to enforce her will, it was essen-tial that Granuaile lead by example, enduring and outdoing her men, as a later poem testifies regarding her attack on the castle of Renvyle:

> No braver seaman took a deck in hurricane or squalls
> Since Grace O'Malley battered down old Currath castle walls.[6]

It was undoubtedly her strength of character, charisma, abso-lute courage, adaptability and self-belief that propelled Granuaile into a position of leadership during the most turbu-lent decades in the history of her country.

Elizabeth I, Queen of England (National Library of Ireland).

Across the Irish Sea another woman was preparing to assume the role of leader in a man's world. She was to excel and be immortalised as the greatest of England's monarchs. Her impact on Ireland would leave an indelible mark and would destroy forever the society that nurtured and sustained Granuaile.

Elizabeth I assumed the throne in November 1558 and commenced her long and powerful reign, which was to end with Ireland brought to heel, the might of Spain shattered, and the security of England — the yardstick of her policies — achieved. It was a time of dangerous uncertainty for the young queen who ascended the throne in the knowledge that many of her own subjects, because of her father's divorce and the fact that she was a woman, had reservations about her right. The implementation of the Reformation provisions became imperative to copperfasten her position, as Catholicism regarded her as illegitimate, without any right to rule. Her rival to the throne, Mary Queen of Scots, had married the Dauphin of Catholic France. The prospect of France and Scotland allied against her was very likely. Although Elizabeth was no religious bigot, in England fidelity to Catholicism soon became synonymous with disloyalty to her, and, as her reign progressed, in Ireland it became synonymous with rebellion.

Initially Elizabeth was to continue her father's policy of surrender and regrant in a bid to conquer Ireland by civil rather than expensive military means. A parliament was assembled in Dublin in 1560 to establish the new queen's title and to reverse her dead sister's attempt to re-establish the old religion. In Ulster, the new chieftain, Shane O'Neill, resisted all attempts to accept English rule. Because of his strength and the remoteness of his country, Elizabeth had little option but to make peace with him, acknowledge him as the O'Neill and withdraw the recently established English garrison at Armagh. In Connaught, the Earl of Clanrickard preserved his outward show of loyalty to the crown and maintained a watching brief on the Mayo Bourkes who, under Finola's son, Richard, had hired a force of over a thousand Scots mercenaries to plunder the lands of MacMaurice and Lord Athenry in Galway. Clanrickard eventually defeated them, killing seven hundred. Richard Bourke escaped back to Mayo where English law had as yet to obtain a footing.

In Iar Chonnacht, however, the first inkling of the expansion of English power manifested itself in 1564 when a minor chieftain of the O'Flahertys, Murrough-na-dTuadh (Murrough of the Battle Axes), chieftain of Gnomore in the northern part of the

Barony of Moycullen, commenced a campaign to extend his power. He first attacked the Earl of Thomond, then the Earl of Clanrickard, whom he defeated decisively at Trá Bán (the White Strand), two miles west of Galway city. This incident was too serious to be overlooked by the English. To overcome Murrough by force would prove too costly, given his undoubted strength and the remoteness of his territory. If, however, he could be persuaded to become loyal to the crown, it would prove an advantage in spreading the Anglicisation policy further west. The Queen issued Murrough with a pardon and appointed him lord of all Iar Chonnacht. In return, Murrough promised, 'to observe the Queen's peace, to appear and answer at all sessions within the province . . . to satisfy the demands of all the Queen's subjects. . . .'[7] The appointment was a repudiation of Brehon law. Murrough was a minor chieftain in the O'Flaherty hierarchy. There was already an elected chieftain, and Granuaile's husband, Dónal-an-Chogaidh, was his *tánaiste*.

This first example of the Elizabethan divide and conquer policy, which was to be used so effectively throughout the century, had the desired effect of weakening Gaelic power and setting native and English law on a collision course from which only one side could emerge the eventual victor. The peace of Iar Chonnacht was shattered as the scene was set for a renewal of inter-tribal warfare, intrigue and double-dealing, with each sept trying to take advantage of the situation. Granuaile's husband, as *tánaiste* elect to the chieftain according to Gaelic law, had most to lose. Granuaile, about to embark on her own career as a leader, watched her husband's status as future chieftain usurped by an outside force that appeared more powerful than the native law that had made him *tánaiste*. As the scramble for power erupted among the O'Flaherty septs, it was clear that the old customs were under threat, and right, by Gaelic law, unless it could be enforced by strength, could be simply set aside.

Dónal-an-Chogaidh died soon after these developments. According to tradition, he met his end inevitably at the hands of his traditional enemies, the Joyces, in a revenge attack for taking their island-fortress on Lough Corrib. Because of his inordinate pride and the courage he displayed in defending the castle against them, the Joyces had nicknamed Dónal *An Cullagh* (The Cock). On his death, with joyful anticipation, the Joyces descended on 'Cock's Castle'. They reckoned without Granuaile who, with her husband's clansmen, defended the castle with such skill and bravery that it was quickly renamed Hen's Castle (*Caisleán-an-Circa*), the name it retains to this day.

Tradition also holds that some time later, a strong force of English soldiers out of Galway besieged Granuaile and a few followers in Hen's Castle. Conditions within grew desperate but Granuaile was determined not to surrender. She had the lead roof of the castle stripped, melted down and the molten liquid tipped over the parapets onto the besiegers, who beat a hasty retreat to the mainland to continue the siege from a safer distance. With no boats to escape, Granuaile despatched one of her men under cover of darkness to the Hill of Doon, to light the beacon there. She had established a network of such beacons as signals of danger. Soon her followers arrived to assist her, and the siege of Hen's Castle was lifted.

Following the death of her husband, Granuaile experienced the discriminatory dictates of Gaelic law. Despite her competence, bravery and success as *de facto* chieftain, the law would not countenance a woman chieftain, and her husband's cousin was elected to succeed him. Her sons, Owen and Murrough, were young men and inherited from their father, as Granuaile later testified, 'the fourth part of the Barony of Ballinahinse'.[8] They were immediately thrown into the cauldron of unrest that the Queen's appointment of Murrough-na-dTuadh had evoked when later his son Teig 'entered into Ballynehinsey . . . there did build a strong castle and the same with the demain lands thereof kept many years'.[9] Granuaile's son Murrough, by adopting the same tactics as his adversary, Murrough-na-dTuadh, eventually recovered his father's lands and the castle of Ballinahinch.

Having tasted power, Granuaile was not likely to be denied by law or social propriety. Taking with her the O'Flaherty men who wished to continue to serve under her, she returned to her father's territory of Umhall, and settled on Clare Island. From there, with a flotilla of at least three galleys and a number of smaller 'baggage' boats, she launched herself on a career of piracy and plunder, which she euphemistically later described as 'maintenance by land and sea'[10] — a career that was to establish her as the legendary Pirate Queen of Ireland.

Hen's Castle, Lough Corrib (National Library of Ireland).

4

The Pirate Queen

There stands a tower by the Atlantic side
A grey old tower, by storm and sea-waves beat.
Perch'd on a cliff, beneath it yawneth wide
A lofty cavern of yore a fit retreat
For pirates galleys, altho' now you'll meet
Nought but the seal and wild gull, from that cave
A hundred steps do upwards lead your feet
Unto a lonely chamber. Bold and brave
Is he who climbs that stair, all slippery from the wave

Irish Pedigrees, vol II

Now a widow, Granuaile was left without any rights or financial means of support, according to the customs then obtaining in Connaught, which, as she later testified, 'never yielded doweries or thirds to the ladies thereof.'[1] By the early 1560s she had returned to the O'Malley territory of Umhall, where her father was still chieftain. As his daughter and, more particularly, as sole heir to the lands of her mother, Margaret, it made sense to return. Clare Island with its stark old tower castle was an ideal base for an aspiring pirate. The castle afforded an encompassing view of Clew Bay, while its sheltered location made it virtually indiscernible to passing shipping to the west. Little could move in or out of the bay without being observed by the inhabitants of Clare Island Castle.

While there is little recorded information relating to Granuaile's activities on her return to Umhall, it is clear that from the outset she was actively involved in fighting her corner. In a petition to Queen Elizabeth in 1593 she maintained that circumstances, on which she did not choose to elaborate:

Clare Island Castle (National Library of Ireland).

forced her to make head against her neighbours who in like
manner constrained your highness fond subject to take arms
and by force to maintain herself and her people by sea and
land the space of forty years past.[2]

She was also accused in 1593 by one of her detractors of being
a 'nurse to all rebellions in the province for this forty years,'[3]
which would imply that from as early as the 1550s Granuaile
was operating as an independent chieftain, fighting her way to
power in the whirlpool of Gaelic tribal warfare. During this
period she also continued to attack shipping on the seas off the
western coast, and was eventually besieged in 1579 by a force
of English soldiers out of Galway sent to capture her.

It is during this period that Granuaile assembled the force of
'two hundred fighting men', referred to in 1576 in the Elizabethan state papers. Her army comprised men from many of the
western clans, such as O'Malley, Bourke, O'Flaherty, MacCor-
mack, MacNally, MacConroy, Clandonnels — all most likely
infected by the disease of inter-tribal feuding which plagued
Gaelic society. That these wild clansmen were prepared to

abandon their own clan, pocket their animosity towards each other and, strangest of all, accept the leadership of a woman, contrary to male pride and native mores, is, given the times, a remarkable and unique tribute to Granuaile. In an age in Ireland where loyalty was transient, especially as the foundations of Gaelic Ireland were undermined towards the close of the century, their allegiance to her lasted until the end. That she was successful at her trade undoubtedly helped maintain their loyalty. We know that she was an active and courageous leader, leading her men personally into battle by land and sea, a fact commented on by an English lord deputy as late as 1627, who recorded that Granuaile had 'borne arms . . . was famous and is yet renowned by them [the people]. . . .'[4]

She is said to have been immensely proud of her followers and to have said 'go mhfearr leí lán loinge de cloinn Conroí agus cloinn MicAnallaidh ná lán loinge d'ór' (that she would rather have a shipful of Conroys and MacNallys than a shipful of gold).[5] That she could offer the English lord deputy, Sir Henry Sidney, an army of two hundred fighting men, willing to fight wherever she commanded, is testimony to the absolute control she enjoyed over them. That they trusted her capabilities to lead them successfully and safely by land and especially by sea was obvious. But to enjoy the loyalty, trust and admiration of her mixed bunch of hardy clansmen and mariners she must also have possessed some special charisma that forged such a lasting bond between them. She undoubtedly enjoyed being in the company of men, of being 'a man's woman', unaffected by female reticence or false modesty in living in close proximity with her men. We know that she indulged in at least one male pursuit — that of gambling — and tradition maintains that her sexual exploits were as notorious as those of the men she led. Sir Henry Sidney's description of her at their meeting in 1576 refers to her as being 'notorious in all the coast of Ireland'. It is clear from the state papers of the time that she, like her great contemporary, Queen Elizabeth I, was given to angry outbursts punctuated by swearing. Given the time and society in which she operated, her characteristics fit the requirements necessary for a leader.

When her father, Dubhdara, died, most of the O'Malley fleet

seems to have come under her control and, as later records show, for a time at least, she appeared as the *de facto* chieftain of the clan. She controlled the passage into Clew Bay, and her O'Malley relations were established at Kildawnet, Carrowmore, Cathair-na-Mart, Murrisk and at Belclare. With Doona Castle also in her hands, she commanded the passage north towards Erris and Tirawley. From Donegal to Waterford, all along the Irish coastline, her attacks by sea were numerous and widespread. Her fame grew. On land she began to accumulate extensive cattle and horse herds, which later numbered, by her own admission, over one thousand head, making her a very wealthy woman.

There are many traditional stories told about her activities at this time: attacks on various castles along the coast from Curradh Castle at Renvyle — where she is supposed to have knocked down part of the wall with a cannon ball shot from the deck of her ship anchored in the bay — to Inishboffin where, during her stay on the island, she impounded the islanders' boats; and the Aran Islands where, according to one account, she came with 'her people in ships to Port Mhurbhe [Kilmurvey Bay] and the battle raged east to Cill Éinne.'[6] In Burtonport, Killybegs and Lough Swilly the O'Boyle and Mac Sweeney clans were subjected to her raids, while her attack on the castle of O'Loughlin in the Burren has passed into folklore.

Her seizure of the lonely castle of Donna on the coast of Erris was traditionally said to have been in reprisal for the murder of her lover by the owners, a sept of the MacMahon clan. According to legend, Granuaile was on a pilgrimage at the holy well on Clare Island on St Brigid's Day when news was brought to her that a ship had foundered near Achill Head. The chance of salvage proving stronger than religious observance or foul weather, Granuaile and her men set sail in the teeth of a gale, across the storm-tossed stretch of water that divides Clare Island from Achill. Almost four hundred years later that same crossing was undertaken in a storm by Robert Lloyd Praeger, who organised the unique scientific survey of the island in 1909. He wrote of the experience:

> away we went under one scrap of sail, over great waves roaring in from the west. The boat rushed down into deep troughs

where there was no breath of wind and only water all around
and up again over high crests where the wind half choked us,
and we got a momentary wide glimpse over far-stretching angry
seas to distant black foam-rimmed cliffs. . . .[7]

On arrival off Achill Head, Granuaile found that the ship had
broken up. Amidst the wreckage, she came upon a young man
caught in the rocks. She took him aboard and brought him
back with the salvaged wreckage to Clare Island. His name
was Hugh de Lacy, the son of a wealthy merchant from Wex-
ford. They fell in love, but their joy was short-lived. While deer
hunting in Achill, Hugh was killed by the MacMahons of Donna
Castle. Heartbroken, Granuaile plotted her revenge. Soon
afterwards, the MacMahons came on a pilgrimage to the
nearby holy island of Caher. From high on the ramparts of her
castle on Clare Island, Granuaile watched and waited until they
landed on the island. Like an eagle, she swooped, capturing
their boats, cutting off their means of escape. She overpowered
the MacMahons and killed those responsible for Hugh's death.
Her revenge still not assuaged, she sailed for Donna, routed the
garrison and took the castle for herself.

Granuaile's determination to avenge a wrong was further
demonstrated when a neighbouring chieftain tried to steal her
property. She set off in pursuit. The chieftain hid in a church on
a small island whose only inhabitant was a holy hermit. Sur-
rounding the church, Granuaile vowed to starve the chieftain
into surrender because it was against the custom of sanctuary
to capture anyone by force in a church. With the help of the
hermit, the chieftain dug a tunnel to the cliff-face, from which
he lowered himself with a rope into a boat, and made good his
escape. Breaking his vow of silence, the hermit informed
Granuaile that her quarry had escaped and scolded her for
trying to harm someone who had sought sanctuary in his
church. Granuaile's reply was unfortunately not recorded.

Perhaps it is her association with Howth Castle in Co. Dublin
that best demonstrates the boldness and daring of Granuaile.
Howth, situated some ten miles from Dublin city, was then the
principal port for the city. While returning from a voyage,
Granuaile's ship put in at the port for water and provisions for

the journey back to Mayo. As a chieftain, Granuaile went, as was the Gaelic custom, to seek hospitality at the castle of the local lord, St Lawrence. But Howth was in the English Pale and no such customs applied. Granuaile found the gates of the castle locked against her and was told that the Lord of Howth was at dinner and would not be disturbed. Furious with such inhospitable treatment, Granuaile returned to her ship. On the beach before the castle she met the young grandson of the Lord of Howth. She kidnapped him and sailed away to Clew Bay. On learning of the abduction of his grandson and heir, Lord Howth set off for Mayo in the hope of securing his grandson by payment, as he expected, of a ransom. Scorning his offer of gold and silver, Granuaile made St Lawrence revise his definition of hospitality. She extracted a promise from him that the gates of Howth Castle would never again be closed and that an extra place would always be set at his table for anyone seeking hospitality. Relieved at the simplicity of her request, Lord Howth agreed and departed from Mayo with his grandson.

Howth Castle, 1801 (F. Wheatley).

Author at 'extra place' in dining room, Howth Castle.

Traditionally the abduction of the heir of Howth has always been ascribed to Granuaile. However, the seventeenth-century historian and genealogist, Duald MacFirbis, in his *Great Book of Genealogies* maintained that the perpetrator of the deed was Richard Bourke, MacWilliam of Mayo from 1469 to 1479:

> This was the very same Richard who took the Lord of Beann Edair [Howth] and brought him with him to Tirawley, and there was nought else required of him for his ransom but to keep the door of his court open at dinner time.[8]

MacFirbis's statement must be examined in the light of the treatment and attitude of Irish annalists and historians in general to Granuaile. While the English state papers and associated manuscripts of the period include numerous references to her and her extraordinary career, her exclusion from contemporary Irish annals and histories shows a remarkable bias. When put in the context of Granuaile's actions and unorthodox life, the bias is perhaps more easily understood. To eliminate rather than to explain the phenomenon was perhaps the easier course for their nationalistic and religious authors, and in this regard MacFirbis was no different from his contemporaries.

Tradition is steadfast in its assertion that it was Granuaile who abducted the heir of Howth, and to the present day Grace O'Malley's name is commemorated on street signs in the village. At Howth Castle, which is still in the ownership of the the St Lawrence family, an extra place is set at the table and the old gates are never closed. Records in the keeping of the present-day descendant of the family, Christopher S. Gaisford St Lawrence, further testify to her association with the incident. They state that:

> Lord Howth gave a ring to Grace O'Malley as a pledge on the agreement . . . it was preserved in the O'Malley family until in 1795 when an Elizabeth O'Malley married John Irwin of Camlin, county Roscommon, when the ring moved to the Irwin family. An Irwin son emigrated to America taking the ring with him. He was a solicitor and married and later his grandson, John Vesberg, a New York solicitor, had it mounted into a brooch.[9]

The abduction incident is furthermore so much in keeping with Granuaile's style and character that as E. Ball recorded in his book, *Howth and Its Owners*, 'the possibility that an incident such as tradition relates may have occurred is beyond dispute.'[10]

While Granuaile received short shrift from Irish historians and annalists, tradition and folklore more than compensated in keeping her memory alive. Many of the stories relating to her have been preserved by word of mouth, handed down from one generation to the next. In 1838, the famous scholar, John O'Donovan, when collecting information for the Ordnance Survey letters relating to Co. Mayo, found that Granuaile was then

> most vividly remembered by tradition and people were living in the last generation who conversed with people who knew her personally. Charles Cormick of Erris, now 74 years and six weeks old, saw and conversed with Elizabeth O'Donnell of Newtown within the Mullet, who died about 65 years ago who had seen and intimately known a Mr Walsh who remembered Gráinne. Walsh died at the age of 107 and his father was the same age as Gráinne.[11]

These folks stories and legends are in themselves a tribute to Granuaile and an acknowledgement of the impact she made on her time and on the community in which she lived.

As Granuaile continued to pursue her trade by land and sea, unopposed from her base on Clare Island, political events outside her domain and outside Ireland slowly began to impinge on the freedom both she and her Gaelic world enjoyed. In Europe, religious polarisation between Catholicism and various branches of Protestantism erupted in France into a fierce and bloody struggle for religious supremacy, which tore the country apart. In England, relations with Spain were deteriorating in light of King Philip's determination that the new reformed religion would not spread into the Netherlands, then under Spanish rule. The Protestants of the Netherlands began to look to Elizabeth for help, which she promised, thus setting England on a collision course with Spain.

In Ireland, a simmering feud between the earls of Ormond and Desmond in Munster exploded into a pitched battle at Affane in 1565, bringing the full force of Elizabeth's anger particularly on the Earl of Desmond whom she imprisoned in the Tower of London. The incident focused English attention once again on the unstable situation in Ireland, which many felt would attract England's enemies abroad. But money or lack of it as ever blunted England's resolve.

However, when the queen's deputy in Ireland began to write about the possibility of colonisation as a means of extending England's hold over its neighbouring island, particularly into the south and west, an effective and less expensive possibility emerged — one that was to have a profound effect on the Gaelic world of Granuaile and her contemporaries, the repercussions of which have lasted to the present day.

The colonisation project was greeted with enthusiasm in England, where younger sons of the landed gentry and enterprising adventurers from the West Country saw it as a means to their fortune. First into the fray was Sir Peter Carew, armed with a spurious claim to lands in Meath and Carlow and to Desmond lands in Kerry and Cork. The claim originated from the Anglo-Norman conquest four hundred years previously. However, in his enthusiasm, Carew also made claim to lands owned by the brothers of the normally loyal Earl of Ormond. This resulted for a time in an unlikely alliance between the rival houses of Butler and FitzGerald, as they revolted to protect their properties against the English claim. On the strength of Carew's initial success, scores of English adventurers set their sights on the rich land of Munster, and a mission of plunder on a grand scale commenced. Exploitation had to be justified and, in the manner and the language of the day, to these pirate-adventurers Ireland was as remote and unknown as the far-off Americas, peopled by a race as alien as the red-skinned Indians, governed by barbarian chieftains and uncouth brehons and bards — a race and country which would surely benefit from the 'civilising' hand of the superior conqueror. The conquest of Ireland by the English was set in motion.

In Connaught, English authority was further extended in 1569 by the appointment of Sir Edward Fitton as the first governor of the province, and by the establishment of a council, consisting of a justice, a provost-marshall, an attorney and sheriffs, presided over by the governor. The powers of the governor, who was also president of the council, were great, and he in effect exercised the power of the lord deputy in his absence. At the same time, Sir John Perrot was appointed President of Munster. The presidencies of Connaught and Munster provided the English government with an institutionalised vehicle, from whence would emanate legislative policies and military strategies to undermine the foundation and institutions of native law. Although the presidency would meet stiff opposition from native power, it was bound to succeed in the long term. By the institutional aspect of its power, it had the in-built ability to survive the challenge of the divided and individualistic native society it had come to conquer.

In Mayo, native opposition to the newly established presidency occurred in 1570 when Governor Fitton and his ally, the Earl of Clanrickard, clashed with the MacWilliam of Mayo at Shrule on the boarders of Mayo and Galway. The MacWilliam was aided by the O'Flaherties and Richard Bourke, the chieftain of the sept of Ulick of Burrishowle. Both sides claimed victory, but later in the same year the MacWilliam submitted to Fitton and agreed to pay the crown a yearly rent of 200 marks. His death at the end of 1570 marked a milestone in the history of Mayo: during his reign as MacWilliam, English authority had gained a foothold in a place that had hitherto been a bastion of

Gaelic law and custom. It was the start of a turbulent transfer of power from the native chieftains to the English crown that was to continue for a period of some thirty years. The chieftains saw their power and ancient privileges threatened by the establishment of the English presidencies, and sought either to oppose the English system, if they were strong enough, or to ally with it if it would enhance their position *vis-à-vis* an overlord or a competitor.

Granuaile's emergence as a chieftain, contrary to both native and English law, coincided with these radical political developments. In many ways there is a curious analogy between Granuaile's struggle, in both the political and personal sense, and the struggle of Gaelic Ireland against Elizabethan England. At first, both are boldly defiant in the face of English encroachment. However, eventually, in the face of the relentless pressure exerted by the English, and the inability of the leaders of Gaelic society to formulate a cohesive plan of opposition, Granuaile's struggle to maintain her power becomes, like that of the Gaelic world into which she was born, a struggle for survival.

5

'A Most Famous Feminine Sea Captain'

By 1567, Granuaile had relinquished her status of widowhood to marry again. She was now in her late thirties. With an average life expectancy of about fifty for sixteenth-century women, she was advancing into the last half of her expected lifespan. Given the dangerous career path she had chosen, it could be said that she was lucky to have survived until then. Traditionally it was held that her second marriage was motivated by material rather than emotional needs, possession of her husband's strategically situated castle being her principal objective. No doubt her choice of mate was influenced by the fact that his lands had access to many sheltered harbours, including that of Burrishoole, where, according to a contemporary account, 'a shypp of 500 tonnes may lye at ancure at loe water'.[1]

This time her husband was Richard Bourke, chieftain of the sept of Ulick of Burrishoole and Carra, a senior branch of the Mayo Bourke dynasty. His father, David, had been the Mac-William until his death in 1558. He was step-brother to Walter 'Fada' Bourke, who had been murdered by Granuaile's first husband, Dónal-an-Chogaidh O'Flaherty. At this time Richard was undisputed chieftain of the sept Ulick and a principal contender for power in Connaught. His territory in Umhall Iochtarach lay along the northern shore of Clew Bay between Achill and Westport. This was not the first O'Malley-Bourke marriage. In the fifteenth century, Granuaile's namesake, Gráinne Uí Máille, had married Thomas Bourke from Burrishoole. Their commemorative silver gilt chalice is now in the National Museum of Ireland.

Richard's nickname of 'an iarainn' [iron] was traditionally held to have originated from his habit of wearing an outdated suit of armour inherited from his de Burgo Anglo-Norman ancestors. It is more likely that his name derived from the iron works on his lands at Furnace in Burrishoole.

From the extant records it appears that Richard-an-Iarainn had been married previously or was the father of illegitimate sons. Besides the son he had with Granuaile, three other sons, Edmund, Walter and John, and a daughter, Catherine, are named as his in the English state papers of the period. In her correspondence with the English authorities, Granuaile mentions having only three sons, and her son by Richard-an-Iarainn later claimed in a bill of chancery to be his mother's sole heir. However, Edmund Bourke in particular was often mistakenly referred to by the English authorities as her natural son. There are some extant documents relating to Richard-an-Iarainn, in both the state papers and the manuscript collection at Westport House. From these it appears that, in common with the majority of Gaelic chieftains of this period, he could not write his name but signed the documents with a cross.

Whatever about his educational shortcomings, Richard was not lacking in the warlike qualities and battle skills necessary to make him a prominent chieftain and a contender for overall power in Mayo. As early as 1553 he was involved in a tribal dispute with the Bourkes of Gallen who defeated him, took him prisoner, and killed 150 of his men. In 1558, when his father was the MacWilliam, in an ongoing feud with the Earl of Clanrickard, Richard-an-Iarainn, with a huge army of 1,200 Scots mercenaries, plundered the lands of MacMaurice and Lord Athenry, allies of Clanrickard in Co. Galway. Later, in a fixed battle with Clanrickard, he was defeated with the loss of over 700 of his mercenaries. By the time of his marriage to Granuaile, Richard-an-Iarainn had established himself by birthright and by his actions as a future candidate for the MacWilliamship, the highest office of power in Mayo and second in Connaught to that of Clanrickard.

Tradition holds that Granuaile married her second husband strictly on her own terms, opting for a trial marriage for a

Carraigahowley Castle (Rockfleet), 1793.

period of one year. If either of them wished to withdraw from the arrangement after that time, they were free to do so. Trial marriage was very much in vogue among the Gaelic aristocracy, and divorce within the Brehon legal system was accepted and availed of by both women and men. As one historian has written:

> in no field of life was Ireland's apartness from the mainstream of European society so marked as in that of marriage. . . . Down to the end of the old order in 1603, what could be called Celtic secular marriage remained the norm in Ireland . . . Christian matrimony was no more than the rare exception, grafted onto this system.[2]

Tradition further holds that when their marriage had reached the year's duration, and when Granuaile had installed herself and her followers in her husband's castle of Carraigahowley, she locked him out of his castle, and from the ramparts shouted down the words of divorce, 'Richard Bourke, I dismiss you', thereby at one fell swoop acquiring a castle and ridding herself of a husband. Their divorce was, however, of a temporary nature, because Granuaile and Richard-an-Iarainn lived together as husband and wife for many more years until Richard's death in 1583.

Richard-an-Iarainn's principal castle was at Burrishoole in Umhall Iochtarach. He had another near the present town of Newport and also the castle of Carraigahowley (Rockfleet), the one most associated with Granuaile. Situated on a quiet inlet of Clew Bay, Carraigahowley is a typical square tower keep of the period. In the time of Granuaile the entrance was protected by a small barbican. It is some fifty-six feet high, comprising four stories, linked from the first-floor level by a spiral stairway, and is surmounted by ramparts and a wall walk. The lower levels are dimly lit by loop windows and include some curious features still extant, such as a stone privy with an outflow down a shaft to the sea, which at high tide encircles three sides of the castle. The main apartment is on the fourth floor and was undoubtedly inhabited by Granuaile on an almost continuous basis until her death. It has a bright and airy aspect and commands a fine view towards the sea. It has a flagged floor, a fireplace, recessed windows and a curious arched doorway on the east wall with a fifty-foot drop below. This had a less sinister use than one might expect, being a loading bay through which objects that were too bulky to be carried via the spiral stairway were hauled up by a pulley. In the south-facing wall there is a loophole through which traditionally it was believed the hawser of Granuaile's favourite galley was attached to her bedpost at night. A small stairway leads from this chamber to the ramparts above. The castle has been partly restored and even in its present stark state it is not difficult to imagine the bare chambers transformed into a comfortable and strategic stronghold.

That Granuaile was the dominant partner in her marriage to Richard-an-Iarainn is evident from the many references to both of them written by the English administrators and military men who crossed their path. At one such meeting it was recorded that Granuaile 'brought with her her husband for she was as well by sea as by land well more than Mrs Mate with him. . . .'[3] Richard-an-Iarainn is usually referred to by the English as 'the husband of Grany O'Maile'.[4] He was undoubtedly a brave chieftain by the standards of the time, and skilled in feats of arms. But his warrior attributes seemed ever at the expense of political cunning and awareness. It was his wife who excelled in this regard. The combination of his strength and her considerable negotiation and political tactics made them a formidable couple. As was customary, Granuaile brought a dowry with her to the marriage, mainly comprising cattle and horses, for which, as she later recorded, she received from Richard-an-Iarainn 'sureties for the restitution of the same',[5] in case of their divorce or his death.

Their son Theobald was born about 1567. He became more familiarly known in history by his sobriquet, Tibbot-ne-Long (*Tibóid-na-Long*), Toby of the Ships. He was traditionally said to have been born on board his mother's ship. De Burgo's *Hibernia Dominicana* acknowledges this theory as the source of his nickname and states, '. . . bellatorem strenuum et invictum, qui (sc Richardus) ex Grania (aliis Grisella) O'Maly, Dynastae O'Flaherti Vidua, genuit Equitem Theobaldum ny Lung id est, de Navibus quia Mari in Navium Classe natum'[6] ('. . . the mighty and invincible warrior [that is Richard] had by the widow Grania [alias Grisella] O'Maly of the O'Flaherty family, the knight Theobald ny Lung, that is of the ships, because he was born in a fleet of ships at sea.') It was also traditionally held that the day after his birth, Granuaile's ship was attacked by Algerian pirates. As the battle raged, her captain came below, where she lay with her new-born son, and begged her to come up on deck so that her presence might rally her men. With the words 'May you be seven times worse off this day twelve months, who cannot do without me for one day',[7] she wrapped a blanket around herself and joined her men. Uttering a ferocious oath she urged them into action, while at the same time she emptied a musket at the Algerians, saying, 'Take this from unconsecrated hands'. The fact that attacks by North African pirates were frequently recorded on the south and west coasts at that time lends credence to this traditional account of Tibbot-ne-Long's birth.

In a poem of praise commissioned from the sixteenth-century poet Mathgamhain Ó hUiginn, and preserved in manuscript form in the Royal Irish Academy, Granuaile's youngest son is referred to as:

> Tiobóid a Burc of the valiant feats
> Of the hawklike blue eye . . .
> He is the warrior whose curving neck
> With ringleted golden-yellow hair
> Is secretly loved by girls in every region . . .
> He is the ruddy-cheeked heir of Gráinne.[8]

Another sixteenth-century poet, the famed Eochaidh Ó hEoghusa, referred to him as:

> Tiobóid, Tower of Achill
> Salmon of Clár Gara
> Emulator of the African lion. . . .[9]

As was customary, when he was about five years old, Tibbot was fostered by Edmund MacTibbot, a sub-chieftain of his father who resided at Castleleaffy in Burrishoole. Fosterage was an integral part of Gaelic life and was considered an honour by the family chosen as fosterers to the son of the chieftain:

The practice was of considerable political importance, for the person fostered could count on the adherence of his foster family through his life. . . . . Conversely, the fosterers would also reap the benefits of support and protection.[10]

Tibbot-ne-Long received the same care, affection and discipline from his foster family as he would from his natural parents. As the son of a chieftain and a future contender in the ruling Bourke hierarchy, his education placed much emphasis on the use of weaponry, such as the sword, javelin and dart, both on foot and on horseback, as well as military tactics. Unlike his father, Tibbot-ne-Long was literate, both in Irish and English, as his correspondence with the English administration shows. He possessed a keen and able mind and, as an adult, displayed a far-reaching grasp of both Brehon and English law, which he used to his substantial advantage. The fact that Tibbot-ne-Long succeeded his mother by sea, inheriting her fleet of galleys towards the end of the century, points also to his maritime skills, which undoubtedly were imparted to him by Granuaile.

In 1571, Shane MacOliverus Bourke was elected Mac-William. Granuaile's husband was elected his *tánaiste*. During his reign, the English administration continued to expand its control over Connaught. In 1574, as a result of a survey undertaken by English officials, Mayo was divided into ten baronies, and the principal clans and chieftains of each barony were listed for the first time. For the barony of Burrishoole it was recorded, 'Burris, containing Owle Clan Philbin, Owle Eighter (iochtarach) and Sliocht MacTybbot's lands, Richard-an-Iarainn chief.'[11] In 1575, the English lord deputy, Sir Henry Sidney, paid a second visit to Connaught in an effort to induce the lords and chieftains of the province to surrender their Irish tenures, take back their lands by the queen's patent, rule by English law, and accept sheriffs in their territories. Mayo had managed to stay aloof from the English administrative encroachment, but the day of reckoning had finally arrived. Sidney returned to Galway again in 1576 and summoned the principal chieftains of Mayo to appear before him.

Thinking that his power and forces made him immune from the English, MacWilliam at first refused to comply with Sidney's order. The lord deputy then embarked on a divide and conquer policy. He succeeded in luring away MacWilliam's Clandonnell gallowglass, the basis of his power. With MacWilliam thus weakened, Sidney sent the elderly Dean of Christchurch, a member of the Connaught Council, to MacWilliam who now had little option but to submit. Together with his sub-lords of Mayo, including the O'Malley, he went to Galway. Sidney recorded his encounter with MacWilliam — 'I found MacWilliam very sensible, though wanting the English tongue, yet understanding the Latin, a lover of Quiet and Civility'[12] — who impressed him with, as Sidney claims, his desire 'to hold his Lands of the Queen and suppress Irish Extortion and to expulse the Scots, who swarm in those quarters'. The result of MacWilliam's submission was that he agreed to rule by right of English law, to pay two hundred and fifty pounds per annum in rent to the crown and to furnish the English governor with a force of two hundred soldiers for two months each year. In return, Sidney conferred on MacWilliam 'his country . . . by way of Seneschalship. . . . The order of Knighthood I bestowed upon him . . . and some other little trifles. . . ', including the imposition of a sheriff in his territory. MacWilliam left Mayo to meet with the queen's deputy as an independent Gaelic chieftain, and returned an indentured English knight. Later, MacWilliam obtained a promise from the English to be created an earl, but it was contended that he 'had no certain estate in land',[13] and the promise was never fulfilled.

MacWilliam's submission had fundamental repercussions for his *tánaiste*, Richard-an-Iarainn who, alone of the Mayo chieftains, had not accompanied him to Galway. It demonstrated that the English were now more powerful than the strongest Gaelic chieftain. It undermined the age-old custom of clientship, the pillar upon which Gaelic power rested, and revealed its inherent weakness when faced with a stronger and united force. It was Granuaile who, more than her husband, realised the implications of MacWilliam's submission and prepared to do something about the situation. By English law, MacWilliam's eldest blood relation would succeed him, and

Sir Henry Sidney at Dublin Castle, 1576 (Derrick).

not his *tánaiste*, Richard-an-Iarainn. Granuaile would have remembered how her first husband, Dónal-an-Chogaidh O'Flaherty, had been set aside as *tánaiste* by a stronger usurper who, regardless of legal right, had induced the English to accept rather than oppose him. Perhaps this was the reason for her decision to let the English lord deputy know the extent of her power and how it was wiser to have her as an ally than as a foe. An offer of assistance, accompanied by a demonstration of power, was as good a way as any to make a favourable impression on the English.

On his return to Galway in March 1577 to quell a rebellion by the sons of the Earl of Clanrickard, Lord Deputy Sidney, accompanied by his son, the famous poet, courtier and soldier Sir Philip Sidney, met with a most unusual leader, as he recorded:

> There came to mee also a most famous femynyne sea capten called Grany Imallye, and offred her service unto me, wheresoever I woulde command her, with three gallyes and two hundred fightinge men, either in Ireland or Scottland, she brought with her her husband, for she was as well by sea as by land well more than Mrs Mate with him. He was of the Nether Burkes and now as I here (1582) Mackwilliam Euter and called by nickname Richard in Iron. This was a notorious woman in all the costes of Ireland. . . .[14]

Granuaile's plan had the desired effect. Obviously impressed, Sidney noted her sea and military power, and no doubt was glad to accept her extended offer. Wishing to view from the sea-side the defensive walls of Galway city, which, as he wrote, he found much decayed, he prevailed upon Granuaile to take him out on the bay in one of her galleys. But business being business, Granuaile demanded and was paid for the service by the lord deputy.

Sir Philip Sidney had recently arrived in Ireland with his friend, the Earl of Essex, who had been appointed earl marshal by the queen. He had journeyed on from Dublin to Galway to meet with his father. Sir Philip Sidney was captivated by Granuaile and, as his father reported to the queen's secretary, Sir Francis Walsingham, 'This woman did Sr Philip Sydney see and speake withal, he can more at large enforme you of her.'[15] What common ground the middle-aged feminine sea pirate and the sophisticated young Elizabethan courtier found we will never know. That Philip Sidney had recently become a patron

of the redoubtable explorer Martin Frobisher, who was preparing for another voyage to find the fabled North West Passage, perhaps gave them some topic of mutual interest.

Granuaile's submission to the English lord deputy in Galway was no more than a judicious gesture designed to enhance her husband's future claim to the MacWilliamship by, on the one hand,

Sir Philip Sidney.

currying favour with the English, and, more especially, by demonstrating her undoubted power on the other. There was to be no change, however, in her activities on her return to Mayo. A few weeks after her meeting with Sidney, she set off south in her ships on a plundering mission to the rich lands of the Earl of Desmond in Munster. The mission did not work out quite as she had planned. She was captured and hauled before the Earl at his great castle at Askeaton. Desmond at this time was fighting for his political survival. Pressurised by forces within his family and lordship who wanted him to preserve the status quo, by external powers who wanted to make him the symbolic leader of the growing Counter-Reformation movement with its Papal and Spanish backers, and baited by land-hungry Puritan elements in the English administration who saw in Desmond's inflexibility and his vast acres a means of making their fortunes, the indecisive Earl was playing for time. Under suspicion by Queen Elizabeth — recently excommunicated by the pope — of being implicated in a European Catholic crusade against her, Desmond badly needed a reprieve. Granuaile provided him with the opportune token to appease the queen's suspicion. The Earl had Granuaile imprisoned in Limerick gaol.

Confinement for Granuaile, who throughout her life never allowed herself be bound by social or political convention, and the essence of whose life by sea was freedom, must have been a living death. Limerick gaol was only the start of her long confinement. In March 1578, when the English President of Munster, Lord Justice Drury, came to Askeaton demanding proof of the Earl's loyal intent, Desmond produced his notorious prisoner. Drury communicated news of Granuaile's capture to Lord Deputy Sidney in Dublin, describing her as:

> Grany O'Mayle a woman that hath impudently passed the part of womanhood and been a great spoiler and chief commander and director of thieves and murderers at sea to spoil this province. . . .[16]

In a letter to Sir Francis Walsingham, Drury records how Desmond 'sent in also unto me Granny Nye Male one of power and forces',[17] as a demonstration of his loyalty. The Queen's Privy

Council was suitably impressed:

> We pray you also to signify unto the Earle of Desmond in howe
> good parte her Majestie and we take it to understand of his so
> good and dewytfull behaviour, in making soche demonstration
> of his loyaltie, as you wryte of not only in words but also . . .
> sending unto you Grany O'Mayle and other notorious offenders
> of his countrie.[18]

Drury ordered that Granuaile be transferred from Limerick to
prison in Dublin Castle. On 7 November 1578, having endured
imprisonment in Limerick for almost a year and a half, she was
taken in chains across the country. Drury met her and her escort
at Leighlin in Co. Carlow. He informed the Privy Council:

> To that place was brought unto me Granie ny Maille, a woman
> of the province of Connaught, governing a Country of the Ofla-
> herties, famous for her stoutenes of courage and person, and
> for some sundry exploits done at sea. She was taken by the
> Earle of Desmond a year and a half agoe and hath remained
> partly with him and partly in Her Matie' gaole of Limerick, and
> was sent for now by me to come to Dublin. . . .[19]

Drury's inaccurate assertion that Granuaile governed a
'Country of the O'Flaherties' displays a lack of knowledge of
Connaught on the part of the English and also the impact
undoubtedly made by Granuaile. That her capture and imprisonment were of such interest to the English administration
in Ireland and to the Privy Council in England is testimony also
to her power. Imprisonment in the dungeons of Dublin Castle
was reserved for the most notable and politically important
prisoners, and convicted inmates detained there were seldom
released. Granuaile's three companions imprisoned with her
were subsequently executed at the castle. Lost to her people,
her husband and children, Granuaile must have despaired of
ever being free again.

Sir Nicholas Malby had succeeded Fitton as governor of Connaught. Malby was one of the new breed of Puritan military men
sent over to implement a more vigorous campaign against the
chieftains and lords who continued to strive to retain their former
privileges and power. For men like Malby, the independent
posturing of the Gaelic and gaelicised leaders in Ireland, the

unstable situation which their individual power struggles created, and their resolute adherence to the spirit at least of the old religion, were anathema to their Puritan Tudor minds. They saw in Ireland's disordered state both an opportunity for England's enemies and a means towards personal advancement and reward for themselves. The methods they employed, particularly in Munster, had as their twin spurs, zeal and avarice.

Granuaile's release came early in 1579, and the reasons for it can only be surmised. Perhaps the tentative peace that had descended on the country contributed. Perhaps the English authorities decided that Granuaile, imprisoned for almost two years, had paid her dues and was no longer a threat. One way

Gateway to Dublin Castle.

or another, she was installed at Carraigahowley by March 1579, when she was immediately besieged by a force of soldiers out of Galway. The soldiers were under the command of a Captain Martin and were sent to capture her in reprisal for her attacks on Galway shipping.

> This expedition sailed from Galway on 8 March but so spirited was the defence made by this extraordinary woman that they were obliged to retreat on the 26 of the same month and very narrowly escaped being made prisoner.[20]

The victory undoubtedly augmented Granuaile's reputation as a leader by land as well as by sea. Her husband was still awaiting his time to become the next MacWilliam, but with less certainty than he could normally expect. The present MacWilliam had converted into a loyal subject of the crown and had become an ally of the English governor, aiding him in keeping Mayo in order. Richard-an-Iarainn's future looked anything but promising.

On 18 July 1579, however, the peace and the waiting were shattered by a holy thunderclap. It reverberated off the high mountain peaks of Kerry and sent shock waves careering across the country to frighten the Council in Dublin and make Elizabeth's nightmare — that Spain would try to use Ireland as a backdoor to England — a reality. With a fleet of ships, an army of some six hundred Europeans, a banner blessed by the pope, and the promise of indulgences, James FitzMaurice Fitzgerald, cousin of the Earl of Desmond, came to unite and raise all Ireland in a 'holy war'[21] against the 'heretic queen of England'. He appealed to the Gaelic chieftains and to the Earl of Desmond for support. While the indecisive Earl pondered his unenviable position, FitzMaurice was shot in a squabble, and Desmond was goaded, by circumstances over which he had little control, to adopt the unlikely mantle of crusader. Sir Nicholas Malby assumed temporary authority in Munster and, 'fired by puritanical religious zeal',[22] burned and looted his way to the very walls of Askeaton Castle. In November 1579, Desmond was proclaimed a traitor, and the dogs of war were let loose over Munster, which was to be ravaged for four long years.

The Earl of Desmond wrote to the MacWilliam and Richard-an-Iarainn to raise Mayo in support of the crusade. The

MacWilliam refused, but Richard-an-Iarainn gathered his Clandonnell gallowglass and, with some septs of the O'Malleys and O'Flahertys, marched into Galway. Once again he plundered the territories of O'Kelly and Lord Athenry as a probable decoy for the Desmond forces to raid Limerick and Kerry. The reasons for Richard-an-Iarainn's support for the Desmond rebellion are open to speculation. That he had a reputation for warfare and plunder was by then well established. His hope of becoming the MacWilliam had been reversed by Shane MacOliverus' conversion to English law. While his right to succeed to the MacWilliamship was recognised and supported by the Bourke hierarchy, the English, it seemed, would back MacWilliam's brother as next male heir. Like most of his contemporaries, his discontent spread not from any sense of religious persecution by the English crown, but from the crown's endeavours to take away his powers. He saw in Desmond's rebellion a chance to secure what he considered his by right of native law. MacWilliam had thrown in his lot with the English. To have a chance of becoming MacWilliam, it was natural that Richard-an-Iarainn should throw in his lot with England's enemy. Granuaile's role in her husband's decision was perhaps contradictory. There was little reason to suppose that she would wish to aid Desmond who had sacrificed her to save his own neck, and yet with her husband's future at stake, perhaps there was more to win than to lose.

In February 1580 Malby returned to Connaught from Munster to oppose Richard-an-Iarainn. With MacWilliam's help, he drove him from Galway into Mayo. As Malby advanced, Richard-an-Iarainn's gallowglass began to desert him. When Malby took the castle of Donamona and, as he reported, 'put the ward, both men, women and children to the sword',[23] resistance began to crumble. Richard-an-Iarainn fled with a few followers to Clew Bay. 'The 16th I removed to Ballyknock', Malby recorded, 'whither Gráinne ni Maille and certain of her kinsmen came to me.'[24] With the initiative well and truly lost by her husband, a voluntary submission, rather than a forced one later, made obvious sense to Granuaile. That she still continued as a leader, independent of her husband, is evidenced from

Malby's statement, as is the fact that she was by now well accepted as such by him and the other English administrators who came into contact with her. She must have soundly cursed her wayward husband as Malby and his army moved right into the heart of Burrishoole and placed a garrison at the abbey, close to her castle. Richard fled with a few followers to an island in Clew Bay and commenced negotiations with Malby from a distance. Eventually he agreed to come ashore and submit in person, but was prevented by a violent storm which blew for six days. As the situation in Munster deteriorated, Malby was ordered by the new Lord Justice, William Pellam, to report for duty there. Pellam reported to England that 'Sir Nicholas Malbie has put an end to the stirs in Connaught by Richard Ineran, husband of Grany O'Maillie.'[25] Malby arranged that Richard-an-Iarainn's submission should be forwarded to him in Munster.

Signed by his mark, Richard-an-Iarainn's submission was couched in suitably remorseful tones. 'He hath fallen from his dewtie towards God and Her Matie. . .'[26] he declared. But while he might have endured defeat in the field, he did not submit blindly and, most likely under Granuaile's guidance, sought the best deal he could under the circumstances. To regroup his followers, the basis of his power, was his first objective. To this effect he offered to 'call backe his followers with theyre goodes to inhabyte the countrye', at the same time intimating that without them the queen would lose the 'rents and dewties' that were forthcoming from them. So that his authority over his followers would not be diminished, especially in the light of the presence of Malby's soldiers in his territory, he sought the restoration of his right as a chieftain 'to take up suche dewties and demands from tyme to tyme as is dewe upon his follow-ers. . . .'[27] With the Desmond rebellion continuing in Munster, Malby had little option but to agree, and Richard-an-Iarainn returned to Burrishoole.

By the end of 1580, however, Malby and Richard-an-Iarainn were embroiled in another confrontation. The MacWilliam of Mayo died in November, and the succession was claimed by MacWilliam's brother, also named Richard, his heir by English law. This time Richard-an-Iarainn and Granuaile combined to enforce his right to the MacWilliamship. They mustered a huge army, numbering '1,200 gallowglass, 700 Scots, 300 kerne and 200 horsemen',[28] to support his claim. Together with the support of the Mayo chieftains, as well as the dubious support of the Earl of Clanrickard's sons, such an undoubted show of strength spurred the English, already committed in Munster, to act swiftly to defuse the situation. Malby marched into Mayo to meet Richard-an-Iarainn, and after much sword-shaking a deal was struck.

Letters patent from Queen Elizabeth, together with articles of indenture, were signed by Richard-an-Iarainn and the lord deputy, Sir Grey de Wilton, on 16 April 1581. They are written in Latin and confer on:

> Richard Bourke, alias Richard Inyeren Bourke, alias Mac-William Eoghter Bourke, that he be chief of his clan and sene-schal of the feudal tenants and followers of our people and nation and of his own clan's and of his own and their lands and tenements. . . .[29]

The indentures detailed the duties required of him whom they refer to rather petulantly as having 'assumed the title and name of MacWilliam Eighter Burke . . . without permission from her Majestie.'[30] He promised to rule by English law, to obey the queen's representative and to pay 'each year 50 cows or fat martas [bullocks] or in place thereof 250 marks legal money of England at the Michelmas term each year', as well as providing food and lodging for two hundred soldiers for up to forty-two days each year. Most importantly, in the case of Richard-an-Iarainn and Granuaile and their capacity and inclination for the importation of gallowglass, the agreement stipulated that he 'would no longer suffer any Scotts or other rebels or enemies of her Majestie ... within the limits of his authority and government.'[31] This stipulation also fell to Richard-an-Iarainn's advantage. With Malby's help, he drove the Scots mercenaries, numbering over one thousand, whom he had hired to pursue his claim to the MacWilliamship, over the Moy and out of Mayo, thus saving himself the considerable expense of paying their hire.

The letters patent and indentures (Richard-an-Iarainn's copy is preserved at Westport House) are significant in that they

Extract from Letters Patent, Elizabeth I, 1581 (Westport House).

Omnibus ad quos presentes litere pervenerint salutem, **Civitatis**
… consensu … et fidelia consilia …
… consensu consilii … eiusdem regni nostri. Concessimus … authorizavimus …
… Willm Tuggley. Bouske … ac … prescriptum ac …
… ac tenementorum … illorum in provincia … in dicto regno
… profirma et comoditatibus que … possidet in provincia predicta …
… non et subditorum … in eisdem degentium contra hostes seu rebelles nostros
… subditorum … degentes … roboret … ducere …
… eisdem subditorum … Pretereum ut patem nostram ac bonum …
… predict tueatur, et foveat. Et justicie … legum … quatenus incumbit
… exigere … levare … infra limites officii … predicte … expressa …
… nostram … gubernacionem … predicti regni nostri. ac per … presidentem
… ad Dublinum. Athlone … Galviam pro causa aliqua …
… nostri … **Habend** … gaudend et … ac teneud predict …
… specificata … concess … cum … et pertinent …
… tamen quod ipse Ricardus … ac bene gerit …
… provisionea … articula … et clausis … et contentum …
… et … **Eo quod** expressa mencio …
… concessio … vel per aliquem … eidem … ante … per tempora …
… illa per causa vel materia quacumque in aliquo non obstant **Te …**
… prefato deputato … apud Dublin … die Aprilis anno regni nostri vicesimo …
… Alford …

confer on a Gaelic chieftain, often in open rebellion against the English crown, a title Gaelic in origin and outlawed by the self-same authority by whom it was being conferred. Gaelic-sounding clauses such as 'chief of his clan', 'that he may tax, exact and levy', and 'that he shall have . . . profits and commodities which he the said Richard has by right possession in the province of Connaught', all testify to the un-English ethos of the office. English policy to extinguish such Gaelic titles as the MacWilliamship on this occasion had to take a back seat to expediency. Richard-an-Iarainn, with the help of his wife, had displayed his undoubted strength and status in Connaught. If a costly war could be avoided by granting him the coveted title with certain English embellishments — such as a knighthood with which he was conferred in September 1581 — then, for the English, expediency proved the wiser course.

Richard-an-Iarainn was also created MacWilliam in the customary manner by his client lords of Mayo at the ancient rath of Rausakeera, near Kilmaine, where MacWilliam chieftains had been invested for generations. By virtue of Gaelic custom, he acquired the extensive territories pertaining to the title: Lough Mask Castle with 3,000 acres, Ballinrobe Castle with 1,000 acres and Kinlough near Shrule with 2,500 acres, together with the demesne lands scattered over the baronies of Kilmaine, Carra and Tirawley. In addition, he received all customary exactions and tributes due to the MacWilliam by his client chieftains in Mayo.

Richard-an-Iarainn had achieved the ultimate office of power with the unlikely acquiescence of both English and Gaelic law. His accession, however, was due in no small part to the intuitiveness and ability of his formidable wife, who gave his more overt methods a double edge with her sea power and political acumen. With the English and Gaelic systems of government clashing headlong, Ireland began to be torn apart. Survival became the spur. Those powerful enough resisted English dominance, while others accepted the changes to such a degree and for as long as was necessary. Granuaile and her husband had won the first battle in the struggle for survival in Mayo — a struggle that had only just begun.

6

'Nurse to All Rebellions'

On his accession to the MacWilliamship, Richard-an-Iarainn moved his household from Burrishoole inland to Lough Mask Castle, situated on the eastern shore of the lake. Granuaile moved with him, at least temporarily. In October 1582 she is singled out in despatches by Sir Nicholas Malby as having been with her husband at a gathering of the Connaught lords in the governor's residence in Galway:

> The Earl of Thomond, Lord Byrmingham, M'William, Richard M'Oliverus, Walter Burke, Murrough ne Doe O'Flaherty, O'Maddin, M'Morris, M'Davy and many gentlemen and their wives, among them Grany O'Malley is one and thinketh herself to be no small lady. . . .[1]

What Granuaile did to deserve Malby's appendage, 'no small lady' is open to speculation. Perhaps as befitted her new title, 'Lady Bourke', she outshone the opposition this time in her unaccustomed role as socialite.

Her son, Tibbot-ne-Long, then about twelve, was placed in fosterage with the neighbouring MacEvilly chieftain in the barony of Carra. The MacEvillys (*Mac an Mhilidh*, which means Son of the Knight) were descended from the Anglo-Norman de Staunton family, who had come to Mayo with the De Burgos at the time of the invasion. They became the chief lords of the barony of Carra and, like their overlords the De Burgos, eventually adopted Irish names and customs. Myles MacEvilly owned the castles of Kinturk, Kilboynell (later Castle Bourke), Castlecarra and Manulla.

There has always been a strong local tradition linking

Granuaile with the MacEvilly clan and with Kinturk Castle in particular. There are many stories relating to her attacks on the castle and her eviction of its legitimate owner, Myles MacEvilly. It was also said that she exacted a yearly tribute of 'a bag of meal, a fat pig and an ox',[2] from each family in the district. Her bravery in battle and her contempt for cowardice were portrayed in another story relating to Kinturk. During one of her assaults on the castle, she observed Tibbot-ne-Long lose courage in the heat of battle, and sneak behind her for safety. Granuaile upbraided her son, saying, 'An ag iaraidh dul i bholach ar mo thóin atá tú, an áit a dtháinig as?'[3] (Are you trying to hide behind my backside, the place you came from?) Stung into action by her words, Tibbot-ne-Long resumed his place by his mother's side.

While folklore may well tend to embellish events and people, in the absence of historical records it is often the sole vehicle whereby the memory of an event or person is preserved. In the case of Granuaile's connection with Kinturk Castle, a place far removed from her traditional stomping ground around Clew Bay, folklore merely supplemented what historical record had, it seemed, failed to preserve. However, among hitherto unresearched manuscripts in Westport House, Granuaile's connection with the MacEvilly clan is recorded in a somewhat different, but nonetheless fascinating, light. Among the manuscripts is a deed, dated 20 May 1582, and signed (his mark) by 'Myele Mc Breyone alias MacEville, chiefe of his name'.[4] In it Myles MacEvilly grants to Richard-an-Iarainn in trust:

> to the use and behoffe of my foster sonn Thibbot Bourk . . . The castle and Bawne and ten quarters of land to me belonging of and in Kintourk. . . . The castle Bawne towne and eight quarters of land of Castlecarry and the four quarters of land of Ballykally. The castle towne and barbikan and foure quarters of lands of Moynulla . . . together with all the messuages buildings orchards gardynes moores meddowes feedinge pastures woodes and underwoods watter courses fishinges emollements and other hereditaments. . . .[5]

All this the MacEvilly chieftain conferred on Granuaile's son 'for and in consideration of a certaine some of money . . . and also for other good causes and consideration . . . be the connsent of me sonnes and cousins.' While fosterage often commanded extreme degrees of affinity, friendship and indebtedness, it seems extraordinary that a chieftain would willingly, even in consideration of a 'some of money', grant clan property to a foster son, albeit the son of his overlord. The fear of being dispossessed by outsiders, such as the wave of English adventurers who were making their way into Mayo, the need for the protection of his overlord, or relief from financial pressure, may have been contributory factors to MacEvilly's action. While Tibbot-ne-Long, still under age, did not obtain access to the MacEvilly properties until the close of the century, the deed served as a device by which Granuaile's son acquired most of the clan MacEvilly property in the barony of Carra. This included Kinturk Castle where he lived for the latter part of his life. The deed may be the basis for the legends relating to Granuaile's attacks on Kinturk — Tibbot-ne-Long was still a minor on the death of his father, and Granuaile may well have attempted to effect MacEvilly's grant forcibly on her son's behalf.

Kinturk Castle.

As the MacWilliam, Richard-an-Iarainn attained his life's ambition. His agreement with the English and the continued presence of a complement of Malby's soldiers in his territory did not deter him or Granuaile from enjoying the traditional benefits and status the MacWilliamship bestowed, or from settling old scores. In May 1582, using Malby's troops under the pretext of collecting the rent due to the crown, Richard-an-Iarainn, in time-honoured tradition, invaded the territory of his rival for the MacWilliamship, Richard MacOliverus. A fight erupted and up to twenty of Richard MacOliverus's followers were slain, including his son. Suspicious of Richard-an-Iarainn's motives but powerless to stop him, all the English could do was order him 'to give either of his sons, Walter or Edmund,'[6] as a pledge for his future conduct.

Later in January 1583, Richard-an-Iarainn and Granuaile showed a marked reluctance to pay the rent they owed as part of the deal made with the crown for the MacWilliamship. Malby's collector, Theobald Dillon, wrote to the queen's secretary, Sir Francis Walsingham, about his encounter with them:

> I went ther hence towardes the plas wher M'William was, who met me and his wyfe Grayn Ny Mayle with all their force, and did swer they wolde hav my lyfe for comyng soo furr into ther countrie and specialie his wyfe wold fyght with me before she was half a myle nier me. . . .[7]

Neither the central role played by Granuaile in the affairs of her husband's office, nor her fiery and daring disposition, was lost on Dillon. The extent of their combined forces was commented on also by the tax collector:

> I being but a C [100] and fyftie [50] foot men and fyftie horse-men, they were contentid to yealde, although they were afar greater in number. . . .[8]

Even allowing for Dillon's desire to exaggerate his own daring, their force was substantial.

As aristocratic leaders with treasured pedigrees linking them to remote kings and warrior chieftains, Gaelic-born leaders like Granuaile and her husband would have found English petty officials, such as Dillon, beneath them in status. To have to endure the insolence of such brash, avaricious and low-born officials was anathema to their pride and provoked their anger, as much as did the dissolution of their power. As part of the machinery set in motion to undermine, overthrow and replace a culture and a political system that were foreign and reprehensible to their English minds, these administrators and military men, with few exceptions, presented to the Gaelic chieftains they came to overthrow the least attractive and bullying face of English colonialism. As ever, to justify the conqueror's exploitation, inferiority and fault had to be shown to be found in the people and in the customs of the country they had come to conquer. Refusing to deal with such servitors as Dillon, Granuaile and her husband would deign to do business only with the governor:

> M'William and Shee came to Sir Nicholas to agre with hym for 600 marks of areradges [arrears] due upon ther countrie, which they thought never to pay.[9]

Richard-an-Iarainn did not live long to enjoy the fruits of his hard-won honours as the MacWilliam. On 30 April 1583, he died, despite the turmoil of his life, of natural causes. The Four Masters in recording his death described him as:

> a plundering, warlike, unquiet and rebellious man, who had often forced the gap of danger upon his enemies and upon whom it was frequently forced. . . .[10]

His was the last appointment to the MacWilliamship according to the Brehon custom of tanistry. His rival, Richard Mac-Oliverus, succeeded to the title, but his appointment was hotly contested by the elders of Richard-an-Iarainn's more senior sept. Malby came with a large army and spoiled the two Owles and 'burned and totally destroyed Cathair-na-Mart'.[11] Eventually, opposition to the appointment abated for a time.

Despite their personal and at times political differences, Richard-an-Iarainn was a worthy and suitable consort for Granuaile. While often forced into playing a supporting role to her more flamboyant and politic ways, they seem to have been a well-matched couple who together, as well as in their individual roles, made a major impact on events. Richard-an-

Iarainn was content with and even encouraged his wife's unusual role, and his standing in the male-dominated society of Gaelic Ireland seems to have been undiminished by her unorthodox ways. In an age that was more male-oriented than most, Richard-an-Iarainn emerges as a man sufficiently liberated from the shackles of misplaced male pride to have acknowledged, encouraged and capitalised on his wife's ability and success.

On the death of her husband, Granuaile, according to her own testimony,

> gathered together all her own followers and with 1000 head of cows and mares departed and became a dweller in Carrikahowley in Borosowle.[12]

Mindful of what had happened on the death of her first husband, Granuaile quickly established claim to one-third of her second husband's property. Her continued independence during their marriage is further reiterated in her statement that she 'gathered together all her own followers'. Tibbot-ne-Long, then almost sixteen, left the fosterage of MacEvilly and entered into his inheritance, his father's estate in nearby Burrishoole, which he shared for a time with his half-brothers, Edmund and Walter. Granuaile was fifty-three and seemed set to continue in her role as an acknowledged leader.

The English governor of Connaught, Sir Nicholas Malby, died the following year. During the period of his governorship major changes had occurred in the province. He oversaw the extension of the English administration throughout the province, culminating in the introduction of a process of rent-paying in lieu of power for the chieftains, and the imposition of the contentious issue of 'cess', whereby the chieftains had to maintain a specified number of English soldiers in their territories. Legal sessions were being held, and English legal practice was being enforced, especially in the trial and punishment of malefactors. While English law was not practised widely throughout the province, Malby had laid the foundations for its future extension. Well might the Irish annalists record his death with the epitaph that 'he placed all Connaught under bondage.'[13] Elsewhere in the country the Desmond rebellion had finally petered out with the slaying of the Earl of Desmond in the woods of Glenageenty, near Tralee, in November 1583. For a short time an exhausted peace descended on the country.

John Browne, the newly appointed sheriff of Co. Mayo and, as he wrote, 'the first Englishe man that in the memory of man hathe settled hymselfe to dwelle in the countie of Mayo',[14] reported:

> that Connaught standeth on good terms and the people live and keep their goods in more safety and travel with less fear and in less danger than in any other part of Ireland.[15]

But it was an uneasy peace, and since the English administration continued to undermine the power and privileges of the native chieftains, repercussions were inevitable. In 1584 Sir John Perrot was appointed lord deputy, and Sir Richard Bingham became the new governor of Connaught. The appointment of these two men was to prove a milestone in the history of Connaught. Diametrically opposed to each other on both a personal and a political basis, the methods they employed in their dealings with the Connaught chieftains were equally divergent. A policy of conciliation by Perrot contrasted with a policy of the sword by Bingham, which was destined to bring him into direct confrontation with almost every Gaelic leader in Connaught, including, and especially, Granuaile.

Richard Bingham came to Ireland with sound military credentials. Born in Dorset, from his youth he had been trained in military service. He served in Scotland, at the famous Battle of Lepanto against the Turks, in France and in the Netherlands. He was in the army of Grey de Wilton at Smerwick Harbour when the ragged army which had come to aid the revolt of James FitzMaurice Fitzgerald was unconditionally slain. He was fifty-six when he was appointed governor of Connaught. Described as 'a man eminent both for spirit and martial knowledge, but of very small stature',[16] his narrow visage, accentuated by a pointed, neatly trimmed beard and dispassionate eyes, proclaimed a narrow and inflexible personality and a zealousness for duty. 'The Irish were never tamed with words but with swords,'[17] was his opinion, and one which he diligently sought to put into practice during his tenure as governor of Connaught.

Sir Richard Bingham.

Bingham's harsh reign must, however, be examined within the context of the conditions and attitudes pertaining. Popular opinion has painted him a villain, the 'Flail of Connaught', the executioner of innocent women and children, but he was no more cruel than his contemporaries. The brutal methods he

Letter in Bingham's hand with Granuaile's name in margin.

employed in subduing Mayo are usually attributed to his individual brand of cruelty, instead of being the accepted rules of
sixteenth-century warfare, reinforced by his own racist attitudes towards the Irish. Bingham's singular failing was his
inability to adapt English policies to the realities of Gaelic
Connaught. It could be said that his thoroughness and inflexibility as an administrator, coupled with a narrow perception of
duty, made it impossible for him to convert the Gaelic chieftains to English ways without resorting to force. At the same
time, his relative honesty as an official of the crown assured for
him the ill-will and envy of his fellow administrators.

In Munster, the English had reaped the high price of the rebellion of Gaelic leaders such as the Earl of Desmond. The
ruthless and systematic destruction of the countryside by both
sides in the conflict had resulted in what the poet Edmund
Spenser vividly described as 'a most populous and plentiful
country suddenly void of man or beast,'[18] and a poor return on
the Crown's substantial expenditure. Rather than repeat the
experience of Munster, Elizabeth I was not averse to inducing
rather than coercing the chieftains of Connaught to abandon

their independent status and clientship powers over their sub-chieftains, and adopt English law and customs. Weary of the desultory conflict over succession and privilege, and conscious that time had caught up with the outmoded structures and customs whereby they ruled their lordships, many chieftains were willing to seek title to their position and estate by English law.

In 1585, Perrot introduced a formula known as the Composition of Connaught, which sought not only the continuance of the 'surrender and regrant' policy of Henry VIII, but an extension of English control over other issues hitherto governed by Gaelic law and custom. It sought to abolish the age-old exactions and tributes paid to the chieftains by their sub-lords, as well as the English levy of 'cess'. In its place, a fixed rent of ten English shillings or one Irish mark on each quarter of tillage and pastureland would be payable to the English crown by the chieftains, and a similar rent payable to the chieftains by their followers. A specified amount of land was to be left rent-free to each chieftain. To eliminate the system of clientship, every chieftain was to be responsible only for his own sept. Primogeniture was to replace the native election and tanistry custom.

For the Bourkes of Mayo, the Composition effectively ended the MacWilliamship. While MacWilliams were elected up to the close of the century by various dissatisfied factions, the title never again commanded the same power, prestige and privilege. To the holder of the office by English law, it brought security of tenure and inheritance of the title by his eldest male heir. To those denied access to the title by means of Gaelic law, it provided the focal point for future rebellion against the English. Perhaps hopeful that Tibbot-ne-Long would one day have succeeded his father to the title, Granuaile must undoubtedly have viewed the Composition of Connaught as a reversal, although it was duly signed by all the principal chieftains in Mayo. It was signed on behalf of Tibbot-ne-Long and his half-brother Edmund by the chieftain of the sept Ulick, Edmund Bourke of Castlebar, by Gaelic law the *tánaiste* to the MacWilliam.

Problems of a more personal and pressing nature were

occupying Granuaile at this time. Sir Richard Bingham captured Tibbot-ne-Long and sent him as a hostage to the house of his brother, George Bingham, then sheriff of Sligo. Tibbot-ne-Long lived with the sheriff and his family at Ballymote Castle for about a year. Although confined against his will, he was treated well during his captivity. It was expressed English policy of the period that the sons of the Gaelic aristocracy in captivity should be educated and be made dress according to English custom in the hope that they might conform to English ways. It would take more than a brief indoctrination for Tibbot-ne-Long to be transformed from a Gaelic chieftain to an Anglicised lord, but the process had been set in motion. During his captivity, he was sufficiently instructed in English ways to learn to speak and write English, a fact commented on by Queen Elizabeth, and evidenced in his letters and despatches preserved among the Elizabethan state papers.

Around 1584, Tibbot-ne-Long married Maeve O'Connor Sligo — 'Meadhbh of the yellow-gold hair, daughter of Cathal',[19] as one sixteenth-century poet described her. She was the sister of Tibbot-ne-Long's future ally, Sir Dónal O'Connor Sligo. The family was one of the three branches of the royal O'Connor family, once kings of Connaught and High Kings of Ireland. By the sixteenth century they ruled an area corresponding to the present-day Co. Sligo. The lordship was strategically situated between Ulster and Connaught. To the north lay the extensive territory of the O'Donnell chieftains of Tirconail, who claimed overlordship of Sligo. Through alliances with O'Donnell enemies, the O'Connor Sligo constantly sought deliverance from his more powerful neighbour. The most recent alliance had been in 1568 when Maeve's uncle had made an indenture with Queen Elizabeth, which he interpreted as a reaffirmation of his overlordship of Sligo, but which the crown later claimed was confined merely to the barony of Carbury. That claim was put into effect on the arrival of Sir Richard Bingham who promptly seized the castle of Ballymote and installed his brother there. Whether Tibbot-ne-Long's marriage to Maeve occurred before or during his captivity in Ballymote Castle is uncertain. If, as is more likely, it occurred prior to Bingham's arrival in Sligo, it would seem that Tibbot-ne-Long's detention was intended to deter Granuaile and the sept Ulick from aiding O'Connor Sligo against Bingham as, in the past, they had been prone to aid him against his traditional enemy, O'Donnell. For Granuaile, the captivity of her son, following on the death of her husband, must have been a severe blow. It was the first of many she was to endure at the hands of Richard Bingham and his relations in Connaught.

While Sir John Perrot was the architect of the Composition of Connaught, the difficult task of its implementation was left to Bingham. In the summer of 1585, he held the first sessions in Co. Mayo. The Bourkes of sept Ulick refused to attend, and fortified themselves in Hag's Castle on Lough Mask, which Bingham subsequently besieged and demolished. The incident seemed of little significance until later in the year when the MacWilliam of Mayo died, and Edmund Bourke of Castlebar claimed the title by right of Gaelic law. The English bestowed the bulk of the lands and property pertaining to the title on MacWilliam's son, according to English law. The Bourkes' resistance flared into a second rebellion against Bingham's government. They were joined by their traditional allies — the O'Malleys, Clan Gibbons, the Joyces, Clan Philbin — and secretly by Richard Bourke, known as The Devil's Hook (*Deamhan and Chorráin*), chieftain of the Corraun peninsula and married to Granuaile's daughter, Margaret O'Flaherty. They were also joined by Sir Murrough-ne-Doe O'Flaherty of Iar Connacht. Among the names of the rebels sent by Bingham to Sir Francis Walsingham is that of Tibbot-ne-Long, who by August 1586 had been released from captivity and had joined the rebellion.

Granuaile's eldest son, Owen O'Flaherty, was married to the daughter of Edmund Bourke of Castlebar. There is no evidence to suggest that he was involved in the rebellion of his father-in-law, save for Bingham's contention that he 'was an open rebel'.[20] It seems more likely that when the governor's brother, Captain John Bingham, entered the barony of Ballinahinch in July 1586 in search of booty and cattle to feed his army, in time-honoured tradition, Owen and his followers hid with their herds and belongings on an island north of Bunowen. Granuaile and Sir Richard Bingham both give varying accounts of what then happened. According to Granuaile's testimony, Captain John Bingham found out where Owen was hiding

> and came to the mainland right against the said island calling for victuals, whereupon the said Owen came forth with a number of boats and ferried all the soldiers into the island where they were entertained with the best cheer they had. . . . The said Owen was apprehended and tied with a rope. . . . The next night . . . being fast bound . . . the said Owen was cruelly murdered having twelve deadly wounds. . . .[21]

In his deposition later when charged with complicity in the killing, Bingham claimed that Owen 'was an open rebel . . . being prisoner with the marchall's deputy made his escape and in pursuit was slaine because he would not stay and yield himselfe. . . .'[22] — a lame justification, which hardly warranted the number and severity of the wounds inflicted on Granuaile's son.

In Carraigahowley Castle, devastated by the murder of her eldest son, Granuaile actively supported Tibbot-ne-Long and her stepsons in the revolt against Bingham in Mayo. She prepared to sail to Ulster to bring in Scottish mercenaries, and negotiated with the O'Donnell chieftain in Donegal regarding the details — a fact commented on later by Sir John Perrot when he condemned the O'Donnell chieftain to the Queen as one 'ready to send aid to any that were evil disposed in your kingdom, as of late he did to Grany ne Male to see if they would make any stirr in Connaught.'[23] Aware of Granuaile's power, influence and wealth, Bingham sent his brother, Captain John Bingham, to capture her, under the pretext of offering her protection. She later gave a vivid account of what occurred:

> She was apprehended and tied with a rope, both she and her followers at that instant were spoiled of their said cattle and of all they ever had besides the same, and brought to Sir Richard who caused a new pair of gallows to be made for her where she thought to end her days.[24]

The governor imprisoned Granuaile for a time while he responded to the continued defiance of her Bourke sons and relations. He had the Bourke hostages in his custody executed by martial law. These included Moyler and Tibbot Reagh

Bourke, first cousins of Tibbot-ne-Long and 'the worst Bourks then living,'[25] according to Bingham. Other Bourke hostages in the keeping of the sheriff, John Browne were also summarily executed, including Ulick, son of William, nicknamed the 'Blind Abbot'. All were accused of practising 'to draw in Scotts',[26] the evidence for this being based mainly on hearsay and on dubious letters which were claimed to have been written by them from prison. Thus Granuaile's life hung by a thread. Her reputation as a 'drawer in of Scots' was well established and Bingham now termed her 'a nurse to all rebellions in the province for forty years'.[27] But she was surprisingly set at liberty, as she later related, 'upon the hostage and pledge',[28] of her son-in-law, the Devil's Hook, who until this time had not overtly joined in the rebellion. However, once he had secured Granuaile's freedom he immediately joined his relations.

On her release, Granuaile lost little time in manning out her fleet of galleys and heading north to Ulster, to ferry in the gallowglass. She was later to excuse her actions by maintaining that when the Devil's Hook went into rebellion 'fear compelled her to fly by sea into Ulster'[29] — an unlikely excuse, but politic and necessary under the circumstances in which she made it in 1593. En route to Ulster, her galleys were damaged by a tempest. While they were been repaired, she took the opportunity to visit the O'Neill and O'Donnell chieftains and remained with them for three months. While the two Ulster clans were traditionally bitter enemies, under the then chieftain, Hugh Dubh O'Donnell, and Hugh, Earl of Tyrone, the chieftain-in-waiting of all the O'Neills, old animosities had been cast aside. Hugh O'Neill's second wife was O'Donnell's daughter. O'Donnell, who was married to the formidable Finola, the Ineen Dubh, daughter of James MacDonald, Lord of the Isles, cultivated close links with the royal court of Scotland. Their son, Red Hugh, one of the famous leaders of the later Ulster confederacy against the English, was then a youth who a few short months after Granuaile's visit to his father would find himself a prisoner, as Granuaile had been, in Dublin Castle. Turlough Luineach, the chieftain of all the O'Neills, was growing old and weak, while his *tánaiste*, Hugh, the English-reared Earl of Tyrone, was growing in power and ambition.

What matters Granuaile discussed with O'Neill and O'Donnell during her stay in Ulster in 1587 have not been documented. In Ulster, as in the rest of Ireland, rumours of a Spanish invasion of England were rife. Merchants and seamen carried stories of the mustering of ships, troops and arms in Spanish ports for an unprecedented attack on England. The Spanish king, Philip II, was determined to embark on his crusade 'to visit the censure of God upon a middle-aged female',[30] and free England from heresy. The religious aspirations of the king's armada would have cut little ice with the Gaelic chieftains, but the political fall-out for Ireland and for themselves *vis-à-vis* the English was a different matter. The Ulster chieftains doubtless heard from Granuaile a first-hand account of Bingham's rule in Connaught and of his attempts to curb the power of the Gaelic chieftains there. With the intuition that was their hallmark, O'Neill and O'Donnell realised that the experiences of Munster and Connaught would inevitably be visited on them in Ulster unless English control in Ireland could be reversed. To date, no deterrent appeared likely.

In Mayo, Bingham executed by martial law the main contender for the MacWilliamship, the aged Edmund Bourke of Castlebar. In late September he defeated the huge force of Scots mercenaries who, with Granuaile's galleys out of commission, had made their own way by land into Mayo. On the banks of the Moy, Bingham routed them into the river where 1,400 were accounted as having been killed or drowned. The rebellion collapsed and the Bourkes sued for peace. In May 1587, Elizabeth I ordered Bingham for service in Flanders. Seizing her chance, Granuaile set out for Dublin determined to take advantage of Bingham's absence and of the antagonism, now public knowledge, that existed between him and the Lord deputy. Bingham's enemies rather than his allies were more likely to receive a hearing from Perrot. In Dublin, according to her testimony, she received 'her Majesty's pardon by Sir John Perrot'.[31] The pardon, preserved in the Elizabethan Fiants, also granted pardon for past offences against the crown to Granuaile's sons, Murrough O'Flaherty, Tibbot-ne-Long and to

'Margaret O'Flahertie daughter of Grany'.[32] Granuaile's shrewdness had paid dividends in the short term at least. She later claimed that on her return from Dublin, she lived 'in Connaught a farmer's life . . . and did give over her former trade of maintenance by sea and land.'[33] In fact, with Bingham out of the picture, she acquired additional galleys and resumed her seafaring enterprises with renewed vigour.

7

'A Notable Traitoress'

On the evening of 29 July 1588 the long-threatened Spanish Armada was sighted off the Lizard. From beacon to beacon the news was relayed across England that King Philip's meticulously planned crusade against his 'heretic' sister-in-law had become a reality. The 'invincible' armada of 134 ships and over 30,000 men, commanded by the flower of Spanish aristocracy, moved slowly and menacingly in a crescent formation along England's southern coast. After a series of naval skirmishes with the faster and more skilfully captained English fleet, the Armada ships became scattered. Fireships sent by the English among the great carracks, galleons and galleases wreaked further havoc. Then the elements took a hand. The wind shifted and the Spanish ships were driven up the Channel towards the North Sea pursued by the English fleet. On 21 August, the Armada set course to return to Spain, only to be buffeted by fierce storms and heavy seas, which drove the fleet towards the north and west coasts of Ireland, where rocky headlands and awesome cliffs took a heavy toll of ships and men. In all, some twenty-six Armada ships were eventually wrecked on the Irish coast.

Sir Richard Bingham resumed the governorship of Connaught in the late spring of 1588. His adversary, Sir John Perrot, was recalled, and Sir William FitzWilliam replaced him as lord deputy. As the Armada ships were driven onto the Irish coast, and messengers and spies brought exaggerated tidings of great armies of Spanish soldiers holed up in coastal castles and towers, the English administration in Dublin, understrength and inadequately armed to repel such forces, panicked. Fearful that the Spanish would unite with the discontented Irish chieftains, FitzWilliam proclaimed it a crime punishable by death to harbour or aid Spanish castaways. Coupled with this, the Spanish ships were rumoured to contain untold treasure, the salvage of which appealed to both Irish and English alike. Consequently, the Spanish survivors who managed to effect a landing on Irish soil, in the main, received a less than hospitable reception.

It was estimated that five ships were wrecked on Mayo's jagged coastline and that many of the survivors were summarily killed by treasure-seeking tribesmen. Given the remoteness and inaccessibility of the region, the inaccuracies — both deliberate and inadvertent — of English accounts, and the distinct lack of information from an Irish perspective, it is virtually impossible to assess the true story behind many of these wrecks. The single most controversial incident occurred on Clare Island where around 22 September a huge ship, the square-rigged, cumbersome, converted merchantman, *El Gran Grin*, of some 1,160 tons, carrying 329 men and 28 guns when she sailed for England, was driven helplessly before the wind towards Clew Bay. With no space to manoeuvre she drifted onto Clare Island towards the cliffs on the southwest side, and was presumed to have been wrecked. English accounts record that her commander, Don Pedro de Mendoza, and about one hundred of the crew scrambled to safety but were eventually killed on the orders of Dubhdara Rua O'Malley. The remainder of the crew were drowned.

The facts regarding the wreck and supposed massacre are scanty. That *El Gran Grin* was driven towards the island is most likely true. That she was wrecked there and that her commander and crew were killed by the islanders is less certain. There is no deep-rooted tradition on the island of such a massacre having taken place. The O'Malleys, in particular, had been well used to piloting and trading with the Spanish for generations. Only the English accounts testify to the massacre, and these must be viewed in the context in which they were written.

A contemporary view of the Armada formation.

On the other hand, the presence of some one hundred foreigners on Clare Island would undoubtedly have put the islanders under extreme pressure. Plunder and wrecking were part and parcel of seafaring life everywhere, and the O'Malleys were no exception to this custom. The foreigners more than likely outnumbered the islanders and, despite their plight, posed an immediate threat. To find food and shelter for so many would have put an immense strain on the island's slender resources. There is a mention in the English state papers that O'Malley had imprisoned the Spanish castaways initially, but that they had broken out and may well have attempted to fight their way off the island, commandeering the islanders' boats, on which their livelihoods depended. Three of the officers accredited to *El Gran Grin* were later identified as prisoners of Bingham in Galway. Whether O'Malley handed them over to the English or whether they were captured by the English bands who constantly scoured the coastline for survivors is uncertain. At this time the O'Malleys were one of the clans least likely to have cooperated freely with the English administration, particularly with Sir Richard Bingham. One way or another, whether the Spaniards were massacred by the O'Malleys, as the English reports claim, or were secretly taken off the island by them, either to a safe haven such as Scotland or to be reunited with other Armada vessels, the truth must rest beneath the fathoms with the many other secrets of the Armada wrecks.

A further complication to the theory of the Clare Island wreck is that it may have been mistaken for a ship that went aground at Fynglass (possibly present-day Toorglass) on the Corraun peninsula, a few miles from Granuaile's castle of Carraigahowley. Some accounts maintain that this was the 834-ton *San Nicholas Prodaneli*, while others claim that it was in fact *El Gran Grin*, which had been driven past Clare Island onto the mainland at Toorglass. The lands on which she was wrecked were claimed by the Earl of Ormond, 'Black' Tom Butler, as part of the original Anglo-Norman Butler estate. Black Tom was not slow to send messengers to Mayo with orders to make an inventory and lay claim to the ship's treasures, most of which by then had been picked clean by the local O'Malley and Bourke clansmen.

Among the reports concerning both wrecks in Clew Bay there is no mention of Granuaile. Whether she was absent on some business of her own or was too closely watched by Bingham's officers to intervene, is open to speculation. The lure of treasure and plunder was a way of life for her and there is no reason to assume that Spanish cargo would have been immune from her attention. Her attitude to the Spanish survivors was another matter. Her family's connections with Spain were long-established and her understanding of the Armada's ambitions may have been clearer to someone who had recently stayed with O'Neill, one of the few Gaelic chieftains who assisted the castaways. But, in any event, there was little she could have done to hide or protect the survivors, even if she so desired .

Derided by FitzWilliam in Dublin for being ineffective in his pursuit of the Spanish survivors, Bingham directed his attention to the Connaught coastline. He ordered his deputy marshal, Robert Fowle, to seek out, dislodge and kill the unfortunate survivors. With her record by now well established, Granuaile's activities would have been closely monitored. That she assisted the Spanish survivors who came her way cannot be ruled out, especially since Bingham later testified that her son-in-law, the Devil's Hook from nearby Corraun, and his son, as well as the Bourkes of Erris and Sir Murrough-ne-Doe O'Flaherty in Iar Chonnacht, sheltered many Spanish who he claimed 'had an intention to remayne in the county of Mayo and that the inhabitants of the same were agreed to join with them. . . .'[1]

Technically, any chieftain found harbouring the Spanish was deemed by the English to be in rebellion, and his lands forfeited to the crown.

It was a combination of the retention of the Spanish Armada survivors and the bad blood that existed between John Browne, the sheriff of Mayo, and the Bourkes of Corraun and Erris that sparked off the final Bourke rebellion in 1589. A controversial commission was issued to John Browne, empowering him to enter the territory of the Burrishoole and Erris Bourkes:

> to prosecute and followe all and every of the said traytors . . . yt shal be lawful for you and yr. said companies to praie, burne

and spoile . . . (giving to them notice of the daunger therof beforehand). . . .[2]

The commission bore only Bingham's signature, instead of the two commissioners' signatures legally required. On 7 February 1589 the sheriff arrived at Granuaile's castle of Carraigahowley with an army of some 250 men. There he was met by the Devil's Hook's son, Richard Bourke, Granuaile's grandson, who objected to the sheriff's proposed entry through his territory. In the official correspondence relating to the incident, there is no mention of Granuaile, but in view of her previous attitude to English intruders it is certain that she would have found English presence at her castle as disagreeable then as it had been before. Disregarding Richard Bourke's objection, Browne persisted and followed the main body of his army into Bourke territory. There he was attacked by the Devil's Hook's family and killed, together with his escort of some twenty-five soldiers.

The Browne incident was a signal for the commencement of the most widespread rebellion in Connaught against the administration of Sir Richard Bingham. The Bourkes of Burrishoole, Corraun and Erris were joined by the Bourkes of Tirawley, the O'Malleys, Clandonnells and Clangibbons. Sir Murrough-ne-Doe O'Flaherty, despite the fact that his son was a hostage with Bingham and was subsequently executed, crossed Lough Corrib with an army of five hundred and joined the Bourkes. Granuaile, as Bingham reported, 'byrned and spoyled the isles of Aran',[3] which recently had been granted to an Englishman, Sir Thomas LeStrange. Her son, Tibbot-ne-Long, and his half-brother, Edmund, were named by Bingham as being among the rebel leaders. Mayo was in turmoil. The Bourkes raided Kilmaine and Clanmorris, taking substantial booty, and plundered right up to the very walls of Galway city.

Alarmed by the strength and extent of the rebellion, Lord Deputy FitzWilliam ordered Bingham to desist from any further action against the Bourkes, and a tentative truce was arranged. Negotiations with the English took place on the outskirts of Galway at Newcastle, the Bourke leaders having refused to come into Galway city. The contentious issue of the MacWilliamship title reared its head once again. The Bourkes demanded that Richard-an-Iarainn's brother, William Bourke, the Blind Abbot, *tánaiste* by Gaelic custom, should be restored to the title, and that Richard Bingham should be removed as governor of Connaught. Many in the English administration, including FitzWilliam, were in agreement with the second of their demands, which simply mirrored the conspiracy then afoot among Bingham's colleagues in the Irish service to have him removed from office.

Queen Elizabeth wrote of her disquiet at the rebellion in Connaught and urged FitzWilliam to adopt a conciliatory attitude to the Bourkes. FitzWilliam set out for Connaught, ordering Bingham to remain at Athlone. The appeasement policy proposed by the queen was beyond Bingham's comprehension. He wrote to a colleague at the English court:

> Truly I have not heard of the like between a prince and her subjects and much less with a race of such beggarly wretches as these. . . . This dalliance with these rebels makes them most insolent and without the sword . . . it is impossible to govern the Irish people. . . .[4]

On 12 June FitzWilliam met representatives of the Bourkes in St Nicholas' Church in Galway, where they presented him with a book of complaints against Bingham and his relations in the Connaught service. A similar book was also presented by the chieftains of Sligo against George Bingham, the governor's brother. Many charges were laid against Bingham, including breaches of the Composition, quartering of English soldiers on the people, and encroachments by officials in his administration on the lands and livings of the chieftains. Specific charges of murder, cruelty and torture were cited against him, including the murder of Granuaile's eldest son, Owen O'Flaherty, and her Bourke nephews; the hanging of the elderly chieftain, Edmund Bourke of Castlebar; and the execution of the young Bourke hostages, including Ulick, son of the Blind Abbot. The Bourkes made a token submission to the lord deputy, appropriately contrite in tone, and even promised that they would 'forthwith deliver to the lord deputy such Spaniards, Portugalls and other foreigners of the Spanish fleet as are now amongst them.'[5]

The submission was no more than a ploy to buy time. The Bourkes were careful not to hand over the customary hostages as a pledge to the agreement. On the other hand, they had prevailed on the lord deputy to curb English influence and to remove Bingham from Connaught. The Bourkes knew that they held the advantage, with Mayo, part of Roscommon, Iar Chonnacht, Sligo and Galway under their control. Granuaile, accompanied by one of her sons, went to Scotland to hire mercenaries. Their arrival back in Mayo in early September was reported to Bingham, who advised Burghley and the Privy Council that '7 gallies to be arryved in Erris with Scottes . . . having for their guyde and conductor one of Grany O'Malleys sons'.[6] However, Bingham's claim was refuted by no less a personage than the lord deputy who told Burghley, 'that she [Granuaile] shold be gon over into Scotland to drawe over Scotts into these parts . . . nothing could be untrulie written or reported. . . '[7] and added, 'this man Bingham is shameless'. The result of the Bourke successes was the inauguration in October at Rousakeera of the Blind Abbot as the MacWilliam. The Bourkes and their confederates then recaptured Lough Mask Castle, part of the traditional seigniory of the MacWilliamship, and plundered the country from the Neale to Shrule.

As the rebellion steadily grew, Elizabeth's patience became exhausted and she ordered FitzWilliam to determine once and for all whether Bingham was guilty of the charges brought against him. After a trial in Dublin he was acquitted, and in spring 1590 was ordered to return to his post in Connaught to bring the rebellion to an end. He immediately set about doing that in the only way he knew — by the sword. Aided by the earls of Clanrickard and Thomond, with an army of over one thousand, Bingham marched into Mayo and took Castlebar. From there he set out through the mountain pass of Barnagee and into Tirawley. Marching through the mountain fastness and boglands, he was shadowed by the Blind Abbot and Edmund Bourke with a small force of horsemen. The Bourkes launched a sudden attack, and in the ensuing skirmish the Blind Abbot's foot was cut off from the ankle. The Bourkes withdrew and ferried their injured leader across to a small island in Lough Conn. The Blind Abbot's foot had to be amputated, thereby ending his reign as The MacWilliam, his disability making him unfit to hold the title.

Bingham pressed home the advantage and marched through Tirawley and into Erris, relentlessly killing and plundering as he went. The people fled before him and hid themselves and their belongings in the mountain recesses. Bingham's army looted whatever they left behind and swept the land clean of livestock. By the time he left Erris, Bingham had amassed a herd of over two thousand cattle. Arriving in Burrishoole, he found that most of the inhabitants had fled for safety into the islands in Clew Bay. For lack of boats, he was unable to pursue them, but he took retribution, as he recorded, of '100 cows and slew all the churls, women and children.'[8] The rebellion began to crumble. The Clandonnells, the standing army of the Bourkes, were first to submit, and they were followed by the leaders of the Bourkes and their allies, with the exception of the sept of Ulick Bourke, led by Granuaile's stepson, Edmund, and her son, Tibbot-ne-Long, who in June 1591 ambushed John Bingham near Cloonagashal.

Granuaile aided her son and stepson, and her territory around Carraigahowley bore the brunt of Bingham's retribution. While she was safe aboard her ship, her land was devastated, picked clean by Bingham's hordes. The sea was now her sole refuge. With her galleys she swooped on the Aran Islands where, as Bingham later testified against her, she 'committed some spoile . . . to the value of 20 mark.'[9] On hearing that her second son, Murrough-ne-Maor O'Flaherty, had submitted and was now an ally of her arch enemy, Bingham, she vowed to teach him a lesson. Like his peers, Murrough-ne-Maor was concerned only with his personal vendetta against Sir Murrough-ne-Doe O'Flaherty and his son who had previously attacked his ancestral lands, and this prompted him to side with Bingham against them. In an attempt to discredit Granuaile further at court, Bingham reported her chastisement of Murrough-ne-Maor to Queen Elizabeth's Treasurer, Lord Burghley:

> His (Murrough's) aforesaid Mother Grany (Being out of Charety with her sonne for serving her Matie) manned out her Navy of

Galleys and landed in Ballinehencie where he dwellethe, burned his towen and spoiled his people of their Cattayle and goods and murdered 3 or 4 of his men which offered to make resistence....[10]

Bingham cites this incident to Burghley, hoping 'to gyve your Honour Knowledge of her naughty disposicion towards the state.'[11] Little is heard of Murrough-ne-Maor in the war against Bingham after Granuaile's action against him. That Granuaile would take arms against her own son is testimony to her grim determination and singlemindedness in pursuit of her aims, allowing neither maternal instinct nor emotional ties to get in the way. It also demonstrates a lack of favouritism on her part, in that she was prepared to admonish kith and kin when she felt it necessary.

In June 1591 a force of seven hundred Scottish mercenaries arrived in Erris seeking employment from the Bourkes in the war against Bingham. In an attempt to secure payment for their futile journey, they ravaged north Mayo, barely recovered from the excesses of Bingham's army. In the mêlée that followed, some of Granuaile's Bourke and O'Malley relations were killed, including two of the Blind Abbot's sons. Granuaile hurried northwards to help, but by the time she arrived in Erris the Scots had fled by sea back to Scotland. Undaunted, Granuaile gave chase in her galleys, as Bingham reported to the Privy Council, hoping, as he stated, 'that all or the moste part will take their journy towardes heaven and the province ridd of manie badd and ill disposed persons.'[12] Bingham's hope was not fulfilled because Granuaile survived the journey and continued to be a thorn in his side. Whether she encountered or gave battle to the Scots on this occasion has not been recorded. Her actions demonstrate the lengths to which she was prepared to go to avenge a wrong committed against her extended family, and how she in turn was looked to as their legitimate protector and avenger — a privilege and a duty formerly deemed the sole preserve of the elected male chieftain.

With the removal of the Blind Abbot as a contender for leadership of the Mayo Bourkes, and the death during 1591 of most of the senior aspirants, Granuaile's stepson, Edmund, and her son, Tibbot-ne-Long, emerged as the principal leaders in the Bourke hierarchy. Together with Granuaile, they were the two remaining chieftains who by spring 1592 had not submitted to Bingham. In the struggle between the English and Gaelic worlds in Mayo, no likely victor had as yet emerged. Under Bingham, English control had undoubtedly advanced. Yet, as the various Bourke rebellions had demonstrated, when confronted by a Gaelic alliance, it was quite fragile. However, despite their power and victories over the English, the Bourkes and their allies suffered from the prevailing Gaelic malaise — Gaelic leaders in Mayo and elsewhere, including Granuaile and her sons, fought merely their own corner. Their only spur was, as it had been for their ancestors, that of survival in the political as well as the physical sense. They were products of their time and of a society which still nurtured the outmoded Celtic tradition of independent and fragmented tribalism, and seemed incapable of producing a single centralised authority. Gaelic Ireland had fallen behind the rest of Europe. As one historian has written:

> such a life had been an anachronism in the medieval system and there was no place for it in Renaissance Europe . . . the fundamental divergence between the Celtic conception of a ruler and the new conception of the state.[13]

This tribalism, when coupled with the divide and conquer strategy about to be introduced on a wider scale by the English in Mayo to accelerate the conquest there, and which would see Bourke turn on Bourke, clan on clan, would ensure the ultimate downfall of the Gaelic system, unless the Gaelic powers could combine and present a united front against the English.

The first inkling of Mayo being drawn into a wider net of opposition to the English crown occurred in the spring of 1592 when Tibbot-ne-Long was approached by bishops Hely and O'Boyle to raise a rebellion in Mayo in tandem with Red Hugh O'Donnell, the young chieftain of Tirconail, lately escaped from captivity in Dublin Castle. Spanish aid was promised, and the prospect of re-establishing the MacWilliamship was held out as an additional incentive. Tibbot-ne-Long reacted cautiously. The concept of waging battle at the behest and in the cause of an outsider, particularly an O'Donnell of Tirconail, was an unfamiliar one. Moreover, since the last rebellion Bingham had Mayo firmly under control and had established a garrison at Castlebar, cutting off the western Bourkes from their traditional allies. However, on the appeal of the Clandonnells to rescue one of their leaders imprisoned by Bingham at Cloonagashal, Tibbot-ne-Long initiated a rising in Mayo and attacked Cloonagashal where Bingham was holding sessions. The attack was beaten back by the garrison. Tibbot-ne-Long held out until he heard that O'Donnell himself had submitted and that the Spanish aid had not materialised.

The attack brought the full wrath of Bingham once more down on Burrishoole, with disastrous consequences for Granuaile, who was still operating from nearby Carraigahowley Castle. Since Bingham's devastation of her territory, during the late rebellion, the sea had again become her sole source of survival. In retaliation for her son's attack on Cloonagashal, Bingham entered Burrishoole again and stripped it bare of cattle and produce. This time he also penetrated Granuaile's sea domain. He wrote to the Privy Council:

> At Burrishoole we met out shipping, and so continued there two nights altogether. The shipping has done great service for the same had cleared all their islands.[14]

With English warships present within Clew Bay, the secrets that had maintained Granuaile's seapower for so long were revealed. The network of harbours, islands, channels and fortresses that had hidden her activities along the west coast and given her the freedom of movement her trade by sea required were laid bare. There was now nowhere she could hide and nowhere to where her ships could run before the wind, laden with booty, and be safe from pursuit. Bingham's invasion of her sea domain and his subsequent impounding of most of her fleet was a major reversal of fortune and one from which she was never to recover fully.

There is an intriguing entry in the state papers for later in 1599, referring to the galleys then in the possession of Granuaile and Tibbot-ne-Long, which suggests that they had been forcibly taken by them from 'an Englishman of Sir Richard Bingham's, who was there killed.'[15] Perhaps after Bingham's departure from Connaught in 1595 Granuaile struck back, by seizing the English galleys in lieu of hers impounded now by Bingham.

For Tibbot-ne-Long further resistance seemed futile. In September 1592 he submitted to Bingham at Aghagower: 'Tibbott Burke Mac Richard-an-Iarainn came into us and agreed into all things for the Burkes, O'Malleys and Clangibbons to be received into her Majesty's mercy and protection laying in his foster-father Edmund MacTibbott and one Tibbot Mac Gibbon to remain as pledges. . . .'[16] The terms of surrender were severe. Bingham set out to reduce the influence of chieftains like Tibbot-ne-Long by stripping them of the foundation on which their power existed — their client chieftains. Henceforth, a chieftain could represent his own sept only and not the septs who held under him. Tibbot-ne-Long was required to pay a proportion of the cost of the English soldiers who had been brought into Mayo to quell the rebellion, and to make restitution for the spoils committed. He was also fined a certain number of cattle. Well might Bingham write after this that Tibbot-ne-Long and his step-brother Edmund were 'men of no possessions or to have of any goods so much as half a dozen cows apiece.'[17]

An uneasy peace descended on Mayo, devastated by the long series of wars and disorder which had reduced it to a wilderness. Politically the inadequacies of the age-old Gaelic system had been cruelly exposed and as cruelly dismantled by the relentless pressure of Richard Bingham's harsh régime. More than most, Granuaile had been a victim of Bingham's oppression. Now in her sixties, an astonishing age in the sixteenth century, especially given the perilous career she had chosen, she saw the Gaelic world of her ancestors crumble before Bingham's onslaught. The unique role that she had carved out for herself had been utterly diminished and she was reduced to the status of dependent widowhood. While it could be said that time rather than any one individual had finally caught up with the antiquated Gaelic world, Granuaile knew with certainty that one man alone had been instrumental in reducing her both in power and in wealth. Her eldest son murdered, her second son an ally of her enemy, her ships, cattle and horse herds confiscated, her territory destroyed and, most of all, her freedom of movement, especially by sea, restricted — all had as their source her arch-enemy, Sir Richard Bingham. For another of similar age, sex and circumstances, it would have been understandable to have surrendered to such seemingly insurmountable difficulties, to have laid down the sword and bowed to the inevitable. But not for someone who had fought for survival for over forty years, who had fearlessly sailed the wild western coastline, who had endured imprisonment and deprivation, who had fought with sword in hand by land and sea, who had negotiated with every major figure in the English administration in Connaught for thirty years and, as a later poet wrote of her,

> . . . dared the tempest in its midnight wrath
> And through opposing billows cleft her fearless path.[18]

It was not in her character, even at this late stage of her life, to capitulate. In the spring of 1593 in her stark fortress of Carraig-ahowley, Granuaile was already plotting her next move.

8

The Meeting of the Two Queens

Many factors prompted Granuaile to put her case directly before Queen Elizabeth I, and equally many factors could have inhibited her from so doing. The reasons for her decision are evident in her correspondence with the queen and the queen's privy councillors, especially Lord Burghley. The factors that might have prohibited her stem more from a misconception of the political context pertaining to sixteenth-century Ireland and the motivations that governed the political actions of the majority of Gaelic leaders there. Perhaps this single episode in Granuaile's chequered life contributed most to her exclusion from Irish historical records. Later generations of historians, intent on eulogising past heroes, could find no place for one who, it seemed, had 'bended the knee' to 'perfidious Albion'. On the other hand, folklore and legend sought to give a patriotic gloss to Granuaile's meeting with the Queen of England, by fashioning it into a meeting of two queens of equal standing, with the Irish queen gaining the upper hand. Somewhere in between lies the reality.

Political conditions pertaining in 1593, at the time of Granuaile's journey to the English court, were decidedly convoluted. The native system was being steadily eroded in Connaught. As had happened a decade earlier in the Munster of Granuaile's old adversary, the Earl of Desmond, those in power had fallen foul of a determined usurper. The society that supported individual chieftains like Granuaile was dying. Its stagnation, its sheer inflexibility, obstinacy and unwillingness to become part of a world that had swept away the final vestiges of medievalism, had become the trap within which it must surely perish, taking with it those chieftains who continued to champion its cause. Gaelic resistance was piecemeal, undisciplined and lacked a coherent and unifying policy. Most importantly, it lacked a centralising authority, a figurehead such as Elizabeth Tudor in England. The Gaelic code, with its emphasis on the individual rather than on the commonweal, seemed incapable of producing such a leader. Gaelic chieftains were still more apt to fight one another than to consolidate against the English. Mayo's fragmented resistance to English power, to which Granuaile had contributed, had left it in ruins. The leadership hierarchy had been decimated. The land lay waste and bare. English garrisons established in the forfeited castles of the chieftains monitored every movement. Granuaile had suffered more than most: death of kith and kin, imprisonment, impoverishment, confiscations and, above all, the seizure of her ships. At sixty-three years of age, without any means of support, her future looked bleak.

As a product of the Gaelic world of her birth and rearing, Granuaile's quarrel was not with the state of England or its queen, but with the individual representatives of England with whom she had come into conflict. She had experienced at first hand the promises and pacts made and broken between Gael and Gall, followed by the ambiguity and deception, and finally the ruthless subjugation as the situation exploded into bloody confrontation. When representatives of the English world, like Sidney and Perrot, appeared to deal with her in a way that did not unduly dilute her power and freedom, she, like most of her fellow chieftains, was prepared to deal, even to make token submissions. The earlier breed of Elizabethan officials like Sidney were content for the most part to be facilitators of such nominal submissions, in order to preserve the peace and to avoid, on their queen's orders, expensive warfare. But international politics and changing religious and social attitudes in England eventually impacted on Ireland to give a more urgent and ruthless edge to its conquest.

It was the age of discovery and exploration of new lands to be conquered, of fortunes to be made. For many Englishmen anxious to fulfil such ambitions, Ireland offered a target less distant than the far-off Americas. After the death of the Earl of Desmond and the collapse of the Desmond rebellion in 1583, the once repugnant Irish service became more attractive, as Desmond's 500,000 acres, innumerable castles, woodlands, fisheries and limitless rights and tributes in Munster were parcelled out among the avaricious victors. The spoils attracted a new breed of English adventurer. Younger sons of landed gentry, lawyers and entrepreneurs, who saw in Ireland's disordered state, her rich pasturelands and virgin forests, the way to personal fortune.

In tandem with exploration and discovery comes exploitation. The natives over whom these English adventurers hoped to rule had to be presented as rebels, as a race unfit to govern themselves, unworthy to own such lands and properties — a race inferior in every way. If they could be provoked to rebel like Desmond, English law decreed that their lands and properties were automatically forfeited and could be picked up at a nominal cost. The bigoted strain of the new, puritanical, religious fervour that was sweeping England and, to her unease and personal dislike, had infiltrated Elizabeth's administration, added another dimension to fuel incompatibility and hatred between native and newcomer. For the first time religion had been introduced as a divisive issue in Ireland. Sir Richard Bingham, his family and many in his administration in Connaught epitomised many or all of the negative English traits, and Granuaile had borne the brunt of their antagonism, prejudice and cruelty.

It is against this background that Granuaile opened correspondence with the Queen of England in June 1593. Her motivation was primarily one of survival — to get Bingham off her back. There was no one in the Irish administration to whom she could turn. Bingham had successfully crushed the Bourke rebellion, and his success had, for the present, silenced his critics in the Irish council. It is obvious that Granuaile was aware of how the English administration operated and was sufficiently *au fait* with the political process to know that a direct approach to the queen was feasible and was her only recourse. She was also sufficiently confident of her ability to navigate her way through the labyrinthine channels of Tudor officialdom. How her first petition to the queen, written for her while she was still in Ireland, was delivered to the court is unclear. One of her later petitions was endorsed by the powerful Earl of Ormond, Black Tom, then a court favourite of Elizabeth. Through the grant made to his ancestors in the twelfth century, he had recently revived a claim to part of the barony of Burrishoole where Granuaile lived.

With characteristic cunning, diplomacy and a sophisticated ability to negotiate, knowing that Bingham had already fed the queen damning evidence of her long career as a pirate and rebel, Granuaile firstly established her version of events. In the opening lines of her petition she informed the queen:

> of the continnual discord stirrs and dissention that hertofore long tyme remained among the Irishrye especialy in west Conaght by the sea side everie cheeftaine for his safeguard and maintenance and for the defence of his people followers and countrye took armes by strong hand to make head against his neybours which in like manner constrayned your highness fond subject to take armes and by force to maintaine her selfe and her people by sea and land the space of fortye years past. . . .[1]

Then in almost chatty vein she told of her two marriages, her sons, and her own situation as a widow. She claimed that the Gaelic system, as it operated in Connaught, never yielded 'doweries or thirds' to the widows of chieftains, who because of the disordered state of their territories and their constant warring, on their deaths had little to leave in any event. She also took to task the English-imposed Composition of Connaught for neglecting to make provision for the widows of chieftains. She asked the queen:

> in tender considercion whereof and in regard of her great age . . . to grant her some reasonable maintenance for the little tyme she hath to lyve. . . .[2]

She offered the queen 'a surrender at her hands' of the lands of her two sons and also the lands of her two remaining Bourke nephews. Then seizing the opportunity to achieve her main objective to return to the sea and circumvent Bingham's embargo, she boldly asked the queen to:

grant unto your said subject under your most gracious hand of signet free libertye during her lyve to envade with sword and fire all your highness enemies wheresoever they are or shall be . . . without any interuption of any person or persons whatsoever.

It was an ingenious stroke to attempt to return to her old ways, but this time with the queen's personal approval, thereby making herself untouchable by Bingham and his ilk.

While her petition made its way by sea to London, an incident occurred which lent new urgency to it. Ulster was secretly preparing for war, urged on by the twin spurs of the gradual extension of English power into the last bastion of Gaelic-controlled territory, and renewed hopes of Spanish assistance. The English-educated Earl of Tyrone, Hugh O'Neill, amidst great subterfuge and outward protestations of loyalty to the queen, was secretly in league with the young Tirconail chieftain, Red Hugh O'Donnell. Tyrone had seen what had happened in Munster where then, as a loyal ally of the crown, he had ridden with the English hordes as they laid waste the rich lands of the Earl of Desmond and parcelled out the dead earl's patrimony among the victors. Nearer home he had seen Bingham's subjugation of Connaught. Now the English were knocking on the doors of Ulster. Breifny had been burned and looted by Bingham's bands. The whole of Monaghan had been proclaimed, its chieftain MacMahon executed. Next in line to face the English onslaught was Maguire's county of Fermanagh. Still on the sidelines, Tyrone waited and watched the build-up of Gaelic resentment against English excesses, fanned by a new wave of the Counter Reformation exhortations of Irish clerics returning from the Papal and Spanish courts.

Reduced in power and wealth by Bingham, any road to reverse the deprivation was welcome to Granuaile's son, Tibbot-ne-Long. When, in May 1593, Maguire finally broke out and burnt Ballymote, then under the control of Sir George Bingham, one of Maguire's men captured by the sheriff was alleged to have implicated Tibbot-ne-Long in a conspiracy. Bingham reported:

Manuscript facsimile of Granuaile's petition to Elizabeth I.

> Tibbot Burke had even then written a lettre in Irishe to Brian
> oge O'Rourke to raise sturres in the Breny and to hold out but
> two monthes and he would undertak that the banished rebell
> the Devills Hoke and the rest should retourne to Mayo againe
> and with his help mak warres. . . .[3]

Bingham promptly clapped Tibbot-ne-Long in prison in Athlone Castle on a charge of treason. With the air by then thick
with claim and counterclaim, subterfuge and intrigue, it was
impossible to verify or deny the charge, but it served to galva-
nise Granuaile into action to undertake the most hazardous
voyage of her career. Haste was imperative if she wanted to
save her son's life. Treason was punishable by death and she
had every reason to believe that Bingham would not be slow to
invoke the law against her son, as she later explained to Queen
Elizabeth:

> The poor youth of the countrey are so extreamly used as they
> are most comonly executed before they be justly tryed or ther
> cause only hearde. . . .[4]

Her half-brother, Dónal-ne-Piopa O'Malley, who resided at the
clan fortress of Cathair-na-Mart, had also been arrested by
Bingham and charged with the murder of some soldiers. Very
little was heard of this O'Malley during the late rebellions and,
as his nickname suggests, he was perhaps more given either to
playing the pipes or to drinking wine than making war.

Folklore and tradition maintain that Granuaile captained
one of her own ships for the voyage to England, and there is
certainly no reason to doubt her capability in this regard. Folklore and tradition also hold that she was accompanied by a
troop of her hardy kerne and that barefoot, dressed in her Irish
costume, the beautiful, young Irish 'queen' cut an outlandish
figure in the court of Queen Elizabeth, then the epitome of style
in the western world. It is said that it was the meeting of two
queens of equal standing, and when the two women were
introduced, Elizabeth held out her hand, but Granuaile being
taller, the English queen was forced to raise her hand to the
Irish queen. It was perceived that during the course of their
meeting Granuaile required a handkerchief and Elizabeth lent
her a fine cambric one, edged with lace. Upon using it,

Granuaile threw it into the nearby fire, bringing the surprised observation from Elizabeth that it was meant to be put in her pocket. Equally surprised, Granuaile told her that in her country they had a higher standard of cleanliness. When Elizabeth offered to confer the title of countess on Granuaile, she is said to have declined on the basis that a title could not be conferred on one of equal status. When Elizabeth bemoaned the cares of royalty, Granuaile, looking around her sumptuous surroundings, witheringly told her 'that the poor women of Mayo had greater cares and greater industry to their credit.'[5]

It is not surprising that the meeting of two of the most flamboyant historical characters of the century would give rise to such fanciful tales, particularly in Ireland where the mainly oral tradition of storytelling over the centuries would have embellished details of the meeting even more. The factual evidence relating to the meeting rests solely on the correspondence of Granuaile, Lord Burghley, Sir Richard Bingham, Tibbot-ne-Long, the Earl of Ormond and Queen Elizabeth. That Granuaile was at court from June until September 1593 is certain, and in the course of that time she was granted an audience with Queen Elizabeth. The circumstances leading up to the visit, the reasons for it and the outcome, though vastly different from the folklore and fiction, are just as fascinating, and in no way detract from Granuaile.

She did not go alone on her journey to England. At least three other people were expressly mentioned as having come to court with her. One was her first husband's old adversary, the elderly O'Flaherty chieftain, Sir Murrough-ne-Doe, who had his own petition to present, seeking redress against a relation, a protégé of Sir Richard Bingham, who had encroached on his property. Granuaile is also said by Bingham to 'have carryed over into England',[6] the son of Ulick Bourke of Erris and a son of Tibbot Reagh Bourke, who, according to an English official, 'attended uppon Grany O'Maille at her late beyinge at Court.'[7] This implies that she sailed her own ship there and consequently would have been accompanied by more of her men, who may not necessarily have appeared with her at court. Her age, although she was not averse to use it as a bargaining ploy with Elizabeth and Burghley, did not prevent her from seafaring, as her exploits by sea, as late as 1597, prove. In 1593 she was still well capable of captaining her ship to England. The south coast of Ireland was familiar territory to her and well within the capabilities of one who was used to longer voyages in more treacherous waters. Her journey was, nonetheless, a daunting one. Few Gaelic chieftains with a long-established record of rebellion, piracy and plunder would have dared put a foot on English soil. Granuaile must have possessed great confidence in her powers of persuasion to have her case heard, to attain an audience with the queen and to avoid being hanged. Rumours abounded of another Spanish invasion, and the seas around the southern coasts of Ireland and England were patrolled by English warships. The capture of an Irish ship, captained by a notorious pirate, would have been no mean prize for any privateer.

Nothing daunted, she sailed her ship around the south coast, past the Old Head of Kinsale and into St George's Channel, past Land's End and the Scilly Isles, through the straits of Dover, and finally into the narrow estuary of the Thames, to anchor at one of the many wharfs and landing places below London Bridge. There the Irish galley must have been dwarfed by the bulk and soaring mast heads of international shipping in the port of London, then one of the busiest ports in the world. All along the bustling waterfront, ships from Antwerp, Hamburg, Bordeaux, Venice and the Levant discharged cargoes of wines, spices, silk, carpets, metalware, pottery, glassware, pitch, and timber, and were loaded with English produce: tin, corn, coal, and the lucrative woven cloth for which England was famous. Barges, lighters and the traditional wherries constantly ferried passengers and products up and down the teeming highway that was the Thames. Upriver towards the palaces of Whitehall and Westminster, the new mansions of wealthy merchants and influential aristocrats rose imposingly above the waterside. Behind the façade of wealth and commerce lay the crowded, noisy streets of London, reverberating to the shrill cry of trader, shopkeeper and huckster, and permeated by the stench of open sewer and rotting refuse. Through the narrow streets and laneways, bounded on either side by wooden-framed houses, shops and taverns, a constant mass of people jostled and pushed their way: tradesmen, porters, pickpockets, beggars, and drovers driving herds of sheep, cattle and pigs vied for position with sword-swinging aristocrats spoiling for a fight and richly attired ladies, perfumed handkerchiefs held at the ready to stifle the stench as they flitted from goldsmith to haberdasher. All was noise and movement — a far cry from the pastoral setting of the west of Ireland.

Granuaile's impressions of this vast metropolis must remain in the realm of fiction and fancy. Like every visitor to London during the reign of Elizabeth, she was doubtless impressed by the city's vibrancy and wealth, as much as she was repelled by the stench, filth and overcrowding. As one who had spent her lifetime on the open invigorating seas and in the sparsely populated Irish countryside, city life must have repelled her. Her mission, however, was not to sightsee or trade with merchant or shopkeeper, but to barter with the Queen of England for her freedom and for the life of her son.

Elizabeth moved her court regularly from one palace to the next. During the summer months, when disease flourished in London, she moved between her country palaces such as Richmond, Hampton Court, Nonsuch and especially Greenwich. In the summer of 1593, an outbreak of the plague had sent the court scurrying out of the city to the more salubrious air of the countryside. Tradition has always held that it was at Greenwich Palace on the banks of the Thames that Granuaile finally met with Queen Elizabeth.

From the evidence to hand it is clear that from early July Granuaile was in England. Like the hundreds of petitioners who hung about the fringes of the court intent on capturing the queen's ear, Granuaile had to conform to the required protocol and wait her turn. Great formality attached to the court of Elizabeth, and access to the queen was difficult and restricted. Other than the notorious meeting of Elizabeth and Shane O'Neill in 1562, few Irish chieftains were recorded as having been granted access. Granuaile was not the only Irish petitioner at court that summer. She herself mentions the presence of her son's brother-in-law, Sir Donough O'Connor Sligo, who had also come to seek redress against the Binghams. There too was

Eleanor Butler FitzGerald, the tragic widow of the 'rebel' Earl of Desmond, Granuaile's gaoler in 1577. Stripped of the vast wealth, lands and property enjoyed by her husband, which since his death in 1583 had been snapped up by such court personalities as Sir Walter Raleigh, the poet Edmund Spenser, Warham St Leger and Sir Christopher Hatton, the Countess of Desmond had been forced to beg her bread on the streets of Dublin. Her son, the rightful heir, was a prisoner, shut away and forgotten in the grim dungeons of the Tower of London. Her story was a sobering example of the cruel and retributive obverse of the glittering coin of Elizabethan achievements, of which Granuaile had experienced her fill in Connaught.

The year 1593 was a time of political unease in England. The prospect of another Spanish invasion loomed large as English privateers like Raleigh, Howard, Frobisher and Grenville continued to attack the King of Spain's treasure ships returning from the New World. Across the Channel, Philip was attempting to gain a foothold on the western coast of France, and Elizabeth strove to keep him out at all costs. The queen's support of the Protestant French king, Henry of Navarre, against the French Catholic League, which was supported in turn by Philip, received a setback that July. Deciding that his alliance with England could no longer protect him from Philip, Henry of Navarre decided to turn Catholic, declaring that *'Paris vaut une messe'* (Paris is worth a mass). His decision provoked great unease in the English court, which feared an alliance between France and Spain, leaving Protestant England and the Netherlands to stand alone against the Spanish threat. The court circles throbbed with rumour and counter-rumour and with the toing and froing of diplomatic delegations, ambassadors, emissaries and spies.

Granuaile opened her campaign to gain access to the queen firstly through Black Tom, the tenth Earl of Ormond, cousin and favourite of the queen, who gave her an introduction to the lord treasurer, Lord Burghley, then the most powerful man in the queen's service. Referred to by the queen as 'her spirit', William Cecil had served his temperamental and autocratic royal mistress loyally and long. Now in his seventy-third year, gout and old age had slowed him physically, but mentally he was

The Lord Treasurer, Sir William Cecil, Lord Burghley.

as vigilant in the queen's interest as he had always been. Subterfuge, diplomacy, patronage, even murder, were employed by
him during his long tenure, in the mission for which life had

ordained him — to serve his queen and fulfil the criteria she had demanded of him on his appointment:

> that you will not be corrupted with any manner of gift; and you will be faithful to the State and, without respect of my private will, you will give me the counsel that you think best.[8]

For the space of his long career, William Cecil had negotiated, outwitted and outmanoeuvred the best minds in Europe as he steered his sovereign through the traumatic years of her reign.

It was to this most able world statesman that Granuaile turned in her need, and she was later to refer to him as her 'best frende since her cominge hyther'.[9] The queen's treasurer was not ignorant about Granuaile. From Sir Henry Sidney to Bingham, for the space of twenty years he had read of this woman leader from Connaught in the despatches of those employed in the Irish service. He had written her name and drawn her pedigree and family connections in his own hand on various state documents which detailed her nefarious activities, and yet he was prepared to assist her. But before he advanced her petition to the queen, he determined to know more. To this effect, he forwarded a list of 'eighteen articles of interrogatory to be answered by Grany ne Mally'[10] (see appendices). The questions and the answers given by Granuaile are preserved in the Elizabethan state papers and bear observations in the margin written in Burghley's own hand. They not only provide an informative résumé of Granuaile's life, her family and relations, but also give her observations and opinions on the social and political practices obtaining in her native Connaught in that period. She gives a detailed account of her life, especially since the death of Richard-an-Iarainn, and her version of events leading up to her arrest, her narrow escape from hanging at the hands of Bingham, her flight into Ulster, and her pardon received from Sir John Perrot in Dublin. Her replies are always guarded, and she concentrates on aspects of her life least objectionable from an English viewpoint. She adroitly neglects to mention her participation in the Bourke rebellions, her plundering exploits by land and sea, her collusion with O'Neill and O'Donnell — both suspected by the English of plotting with Spain — and her importation of Scottish mercenaries. Her replies show a deftness and cunning subtlety and are a match for Burghley's machiavellian mind.

While she awaited response to the articles, a letter came to Court hotfoot from Sir Richard Bingham in Ireland who had only lately learned that

> there be 2 notable traitors gon over Sir Morow ne doe and Grainy O'Maly both rebelle from their childhoode and continually in accion . . . for notwithstanding that they have many pardons there ys matter ynough of late found out against them to hang them by justice. . . .[11]

Knowing full well that the two petitioners would have little positive to say on his behalf, he sought to pre-empt their accusations:

> if they be drawen to make generall exclamations against me, I do not doubt but your honour will most honorably and indifferently consyder of it. . . .[12]

This damning indictment did not adversely affect Granuaile's chances. Her replies to Burghley's questions seem to have been at once satisfactory and intriguing enough for Elizabeth to wish to see her. That Granuaile undoubtedly had support at court is commented on by Bingham, disgruntled and amazed at 'having bin advertised from thence that some in Court hath comended her for doing her Matie good service. . . .'[13] There was trouble brewing in Ulster, and stories abounded of the supposedly loyal Earl of Tyrone's intrigue with Spain, and of a confederacy being forged among the Ulster chieftains, guaranteed to send shivers of unease down English backs lest Ireland would join with Spain and France in one grand alliance against them. From Burghley's perspective, and despite Bingham's objections, to pardon rather than to punish past offenders, and to maintain an influential leader like Granuaile in some semblance of loyalty was, given the political atmosphere then prevailing, a wiser course to follow.

Manuscript facsimile of the Articles of Interrogatory.

Manuscript facsimile of Granuaile's replies to the Articles, with Burghley's observations in the margin.

Later in July, Granuaile finally received her summons to appear before the queen. Elizabeth was at the apex of her power, the beloved Gloriana of her people, the 'Goddesse Heavenly Bright' of Edmund Spenser's 'Faerie Queene', Good Queen Bess, the saviour of England from the tyrannical ambitions of Spain. For thirty-five years she had steered England safely through turbulent political waters, by a strategy of delay, procrastination, secrecy, compromise and prudence, and had proven her worth and her right to rule. While she may have had the 'the body of a weak and feeble woman', she had shown that she possessed, 'the heart and stomach of a king, and a king of England too',[14] as she told her troops at Tilbury in 1588, when the Armada was bearing down on England's shores. By sheer graft, personality and an inherited Tudor belief in her God-given right to rule, this bastard daughter of Henry VIII and Anne Boleyn, without a clear title to the throne, had won the respect and adoration of all England.

She could be coarse and bawdy, she spat and picked her teeth, was given to swearing, had a temper to match her red hair, and boxed the ears of her ministers, who constantly despaired of her making up her mind. A brilliant scholar and linguist, she had a cruel wit and a razor-sharp tongue. She bullied and cajoled her flamboyant, quarrelsome courtiers like children, and demanded and received their dying devotion and symbolic love. In her sixtieth year, age had not spared even the deified figure of Elizabeth Tudor. Her eyes peered short-sightedly out of her sharp-featured face, her red hair had given way to a wig, her face was a mask of rice powder and rouge, her nose 'grew hooked as a harridan's',[15] and her teeth were decayed and blackened. But what age had ravaged, Elizabeth Tudor sought to conceal by the sheer opulence and radiance of her wardrobe, and she strutted through her court dressed like some exotic bird:

> The Queen's dresses were not distinguished by refinement of taste: it was rather at a magnificent display that she aimed and her predilection was for gowns richly embroidered and sewn with jewels, so that they were as encrusted with ornament as the buildings of the early English Renaissance.[16]

This was the vain, autocratic, supreme ruler with whom Granuaile sought to do business. The similarities between them were marked. They were of similar age. Both were women who had usurped what was perceived to be a man's role. And their respective laws had sought to deprive them both of power. By sheer determination, example and obstinacy, they had prevailed and won. Both were well used to ruling men, and to having their orders obeyed. As a poet wrote of Granuaile:

> She seemed well used to power, as one that hath
> Dominion over men of savage mood. . . .[17]

Both displayed a certain magnetism, which kept their followers in thrall and loyal until the end of their lives. Both sought to protect their 'country' and their power from the excesses of whatever enemy sought to deprive them of it. For Elizabeth, the enemy was Spain; for Granuaile, the enemy was Elizabeth's own military men in Connaught.

Age and the harsh environment in which she operated had undoubtedly left its imprint on Granuaile. Unlike Elizabeth, perhaps the furrows and wrinkles of age, salt spray and wind lay exposed for all to see on her face. It is unlikely that she could have survived her long battle with the elements and her enemies over the space of forty years without some outward scar or blemish. Granuaile's dress, while doubtless the finest available in her wardrobe, was hardly a match for, or indeed a threat to, the opulence of the queen.

In other respects, blatant differences existed between them. Each represented a culture totally incompatible with, and incomprehensible to, the other. Their two cultures were embarked on a collision course from which there could only be one winner. Despite Elizabeth's assertion of having 'the heart and stomach of a king', unlike Granuaile she had never led her men personally into battle. Nor, despite her claim to be 'mistress of the seas', had she ever sailed further downriver than Greenwich. Elizabeth ruled from the protection and comfort of her palaces, surrounded by a retinue of loyal and able advisors. Granuaile fearlessly led and ruled by land and sea alone. She had taken two husbands and, if tradition is to be believed, at least one lover. She had borne three sons and a daughter. Elizabeth had retained her power only at the expense of personal happiness and fulfilment. Marriage had become incompatible with her crown as she told Robert Dudley, one of the first of her many suitors:

> God's death, my lord, I will have but one mistress and no master.[18]

Only in solitary virginity could Elizabeth hope to rule her bickering courtiers, by appearing as a lover to them all and as a mother to her country.

On a summer's day in late July, most likely within the lavish surroundings of Greenwich Palace, these two elderly women came face to face. Their conversation is believed to have been conducted in Latin, the language often used by the English in their dealings with Irish chieftains, and one in which the queen was one of the most proficient of her age. As befitted the occasion, Granuaile would undoubtedly have dressed with at least as much care as she had in 1581 at Sir Nicholas Malby's celebrations in Galway where she had been singled out among the guests as being 'no small lady'. She could not, and perhaps wisely on this occasion chose not to, compete with Elizabeth in the fashion stakes. What was the advantage to be gained from such a display? Far better to achieve what she came for by evoking the queen's compassion rather than her jealousy. It was a successful ploy and one which paid dividends, because Elizabeth later ordered Bingham 'to have pity for the poor aged woman',[19] who had come before her.

The correspondence emanating from the meeting is the only clue remaining as to what transpired between the two women. Granuaile, in a later letter to Lord Burghley, writes of 'the clemencie and favour'[20] displayed by the queen towards her at their meeting. The queen's letter regarding the meeting is more revealing, and is testimony to how well Granuaile negotiated her case. The only unlawful act attributed to Granuaile during the course of the interview was her flamboyant chastisement of her son, Murrough-ne-Maor O'Flaherty, by which the queen and Burghley seemed to have been enthralled, as both mention the incident in their respective correspondence.

The meeting (*Anthologia Hibernica*, 1793).

The queen glances over Granuaile's other more damning activities by observing merely that Granuaile 'hath at times lived out of order.'[21] She listened with a mixture of admiration and compassion to Granuaile as she outlined the excesses of Sir Richard Bingham against her and her family, and heard her, with some audacity, seek the queen's protection from her own governor. Granuaile asked the queen to procure the release of her son and half-brother and requested her own reinstatement to her trade of 'maintenance by land and sea',[22] which she couched in such a way that Elizabeth interpreted it, as Granuaile doubtless intended, 'that she will fight in our quarrel

Granuaile before Elizabeth I (eighteenth-century woodcut).

with all the world',[23] so that it could 'yield to her some maintenance for her living the rest of her old years.'[24]

Granuaile took her leave of Queen Elizabeth, who promised
to have her requests investigated and to give her her letter to Sir
Richard Bingham. Like officialdom everywhere, certain proce-
dures had to be complied with. The queen ordered her Privy
Council to seek an explanation from Sir Richard Bingham
regarding his treatment of Granuaile and how best her situation
could be relieved. In his defence, in a letter bristling with indig-
nation and affronted self-righteousness, Bingham declared his
innocence and dared Granuaile

> to shew me instance of any one that ever I used vilence
> against, havinge alwayes (I thancke the Lord) had that consid-
> eracion of christian dutye as I never sought any man's bloode
> otherwise then by course of her Maties. Comon lawes to take
> away.[25]

Outraged that the queen and her council should contemplate
reinstating Granuaile and Sir Murrough-ne-Doe, both of whom
he had gone to such lengths to destroy, he contended, perhaps
not without some truth, that

> for so long as Grany Ne Maly and he were of power to make
> any sturres the state was never troubled with their complaints
> but now that they are pulled dowen and forced in speight of
> their hartes to submit themselves to her Matis lawes they pretend
> many wronges and are not ashamed to aske recompence.[26]

Rather than discussing the reinstatement of Granuaile, Bingham advised the opposite, adding:

> how great soever any may make her wich knoweth her not, I
> will never aske but a boat of xxx tonnes to beate her . . . and
> with gods assistance dryve her and all her fleet into the sea.[27]

Burghley digested the intemperate tones of Bingham's letter
before making final recommendations to the queen. Mean-
while, Granuaile remained on in London, awaiting her
response and fearing greatly that Bingham might execute
Tibbot-ne-Long in her absence. In early September, she wrote
to Burghley, reminding him that 'hir Matie hath promised hir hir
letters to Sr Richard Bingham', and begged him to ensure that

her 'sonne maye take no harme in body or goods untyll her Matie. pleasure be further knowne.'[28]

Eventually, towards the end of September, Granuaile achieved her goal. The queen wrote her recommendations to Bingham. She ordered him to release Tibbot-ne-Long and Dónal-ne-Piopa from prison. Regarding Granuaile's personal plight, which Elizabeth described as 'having not by the custom of the Irish any title to any livelihood or position or portion of her two husbands lands, now being a widow',[29] she ordered that provision be made for her out of her sons' estates, the amount to be deducted, by the queen's specific command, from their taxes. She urged Bingham 'that you also shall with your favour in all their good causes protect them to live in peace to enjoy their livelihoods'. She further noted that Granuaile had

> departeth with great thankfulness and with many earnest promises that she will, as long as she lives, continue a dutiful subject, yea and will employ all her power to offend and prosecute any offender against us.[30]

Knowing Granuaile's capabilities and the opportunities that such an offer presented to her once back in Ireland, it was a promise that must have sent shivers of apprehension through Bingham.

9

End of an Era

Granuaile's visit to the court of Elizabeth must have been the subject of much interest and discussion among her relations and followers in Connaught. That she could negotiate with an authority greater than the omnipotent English governor who held the other Gaelic leaders of the province in his grip, and could succeed in having his dictates over-ruled, undoubtedly added greatly to her prestige among them. That she likewise made an impression on the queen and her ministers is evidenced by their entertainment of her and their investigation of her requests. Her status as a political leader in Ireland was further acknowledged in the new map of Ireland by Baptista Boazio, published a few years later, where her name figures prominently among the listed Irish chieftains — the only woman included. What the Irish annalists chose to conceal and ignore, English cartographers and administrators were more willing to concede — Granuaile had earned the right to be numbered among the leaders of sixteenth-century Ireland, as valid a chieftain as any of her male peers.

The practical results of her mission to England took longer to manifest themselves. Bingham proved recalcitrant, even when confronted with the provisions of the queen's letter, which Granuaile delivered to him personally. But Granuaile was not prepared to allow her endeavours regarding her son and her half-brother to be negated by Bingham's hostility. According to Bingham, 'importunately swearing that she would else repaire againe into England',[1] she pressurised him to 'enlarge Grany O'Mally, her son Tibbot and brother Donel na

Pipee, upon such slender surytes (sureties).'[2]

In providing for Granuaile and her family, the queen had neglected to obtain the sureties or pledges usually extracted from a petitioner in lieu of favours or pardons granted. Elizabeth and Burghley had underestimated the capabilities of the 'aged woman', whose age belied the boundless energy and plotting talents that had helped her survive for so long. But Bingham had first-hand experience of her capabilities and realised that the queen had in effect granted his most persistent adversary a *carte blanche* to return to sea with her galleys and resume her old trade of 'maintenance', under the guise of fighting the queen's 'quarrel with all the world', despite all he had expended and endured to destroy her. For the moment, there was little he could do but obey the queen's command.

Bingham freed Tibbot-ne-Long from prison in Athlone in mid-November 1593. Tibbot-ne-Long wrote later of the deprivation he had endured while in Bingham's custody and stated that, 'he could not stand upon his legges through that durance and misery he suffered there.'[3] Dónal-ne-Piopa was also released. With both of them free from Bingham's clutches, Granuaile busied herself to take full advantage of the queen's letter regarding her own situation. To this effect, she started to rebuild her fleet for the purpose of re-establishing her trade of 'maintenance' by sea, with three large galleys, which English records describe as being capable of carrying three hundred men apiece. The countryside around still bore the scars of warfare, and the sea was once again to be her salvation. Bingham watched her preparations with alarm as he searched for a way of thwarting her without openly disobeying the orders of his queen.

Later in 1594, as Granuaile prepared to return to the sea, furnished with her newly acquired galleys, Bingham struck. Contrary to the conditions of the Composition, he ordered a Captain Strittes and a troop of soldiers to accompany her by sea to monitor her activities. He forced her and Tibbot-ne-Long, as she later complained to England, 'to repaire to the seas wher in certain illandes eighteen chiefest of the Bourkes being proclaimed traytors were killed.'[4] These were the remnants of

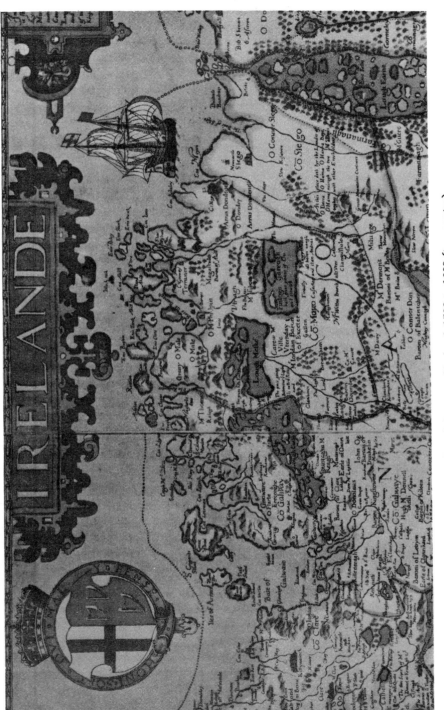

Grace's name on Boazio's map of Ireland, 1599 to 1609 (top centre).

the army of her grandson, Richard Bourke, the son of the Devil's Hook, who, acting as a decoy for O'Neill and Maguire in Ulster, had plundered north Mayo but had been routed by a detachment of Bingham's troops. He and others had taken refuge on the lonely island of Iniskea, off Achill, where the massacre took place. Richard Bourke and four of his companions managed to escape. To be party to the slaughter of their relations must have been a bitter pill for Granuaile and her son to swallow. Their involuntary co-operation was later given as proof of Tibbot-ne-Long's loyalty to the queen by certain officers in the English service, anxious to lure him from confederacy with the Ulster chieftains. It is highly unlikely, however, that they did so voluntarily, as Granuaile's son-in-law, the Devil's Hook, and his son, Richard Bourke, continued to be Granuaile's, and later her son's, most steadfast allies.

To curb Granuaile from further plotting against him by land, Bingham caused a detachment of his soldiers to

> place and cesse themselves taking up meat and drinke after their own serving and six pens per diem for every souldier and four pens per diem for his mann, where they do remain all these seavenn moneths. . .[5]

on her lands. The result, as Granuaile vividly described to Burghley, was the impoverishment of herself, her son, cousins and followers.

Unable to bear the financial strain, Granuaile, her son, cousins and followers were forced to flee Mayo and 'to withdraw themselves into the province of Mounster, where they do remain in great distress.'[6] We can envisage this exodus from Mayo — the little band of refugees, whose only hope of salvation lay in the dauntlessness and the contacts of the remarkable, elderly matriarch who had been their leader for forty years. Their faith in her limitless energy, political acumen and sheer nerve must have been great to risk such a journey. They sailed from Clew Bay southwards, rounded the south coast and up the river Suir where, in April 1595, Granuaile again sought the help of Black Tom, Earl of Ormond, at his newly built Elizabethan manor at Carrick-on-Suir. She prevailed on the earl, as he wrote to Burghley,

Thomas (Black Tom), Earl of Ormond

for my letter to you on her behalf as I could not refrain to write these fewe lines unto your Lordship by her. Though I was verie lothe considering your Ls. Weightie causes to trouble you with her private suite, the declaration wherof I refer to herself. . . .[7]

Black Tom's advice perhaps spurred Granuaile in her accompanying petition to tender submissions again to the queen concerning the lands of both her sons — Tibbot-ne-Long and

Murrough-ne-Maor O'Flaherty — as well as the lands of her O'Malley relations who had fled south in her company. To alleviate their desperate plight, she sought again a means to circumvent Bingham's close scrutiny of her activities, which was rendering her both powerless and penniless. She made an offer to the queen that

> your suppliant, her sonnes, cusens and followers will serve with a hundred menn at their ownn chardges at sease uponn the coaste of Ireland in her Majesties warres uponn all occasions everie yeare from Eister till Michelmas. . . .[8]

While her offer was not immediately availed of by the Privy Council, it acted later as a means by which her sons, in an effort by the English to draw them away from the Ulster chieftains, were accorded the leadership of such a private army but paid for out of the queen's purse.

From Black Tom's letter and from a later petition, dated 5 May 1595, from Granuaile to Burghley, in which she speaks 'at my last beinge here'[9] (at the English court), it is clear that some time between 17 April, the date of Black Tom's covering letter, and 5 May, she sailed again to England to plead her case, this time with Lord Burghley at court. Unlike the formality of her earlier petitions, which are written mainly in the third person, this petition is written in the first person. In it Granuaile informed Burghley that because of 'Sir Richard Binghams hard dealinge'[10] of her, and contrary to the earlier provision made for her by the queen, she had been unable to 'posses and injoie the third parte of the lands and comodities of McWilliam and Oflahertie as lawful wif unto each of them. . . .'[11] She begged him to make Bingham back off so that, as she says:

> I maye lyve secure of my life which hath been atempted sundrie tymes be the said Sr Richard Bingham his brethren and others by his direcsion. . . .[12]

She asked 'for the Lord Treasurer's favourable letters in me owne and me sonnes behalf to the Lo. Deputie and to Sr Richard Bingham,' and craved his lordship's pardon 'for my contynuall boldness'. Her 'boldness' was rewarded when, in August 1595, a commission was granted by the queen and the

Privy Council to investigate the lands in Mayo claimed by her sons, Tibbot-ne-Long and Murrough O'Flaherty, her grandson, Dónal O'Flaherty, son of Owen, Owen, Dermot and Dónal O'Malley of 'Owel O'Mallie', and Miles MacEvilly, Tibbot-ne-Long's foster-father 'with the intention of the Queen accepting their surrenders of the premises and regranting them by letters patent....'[13]

Regarding her own harsh treatment at the hands of Bingham, fate was about to intervene to remove him once and for all from Connaught. Burghley's entertainment of her petition and his intervention again with the queen are testimony to Granuaile's intuitive persistence and ability to have her case heard by those in power in England, rather than suffer the indignity of having to seek favours from unfriendly and less influential administrators in Ireland. But favours had to be reciprocated, and from the time of this, her final visit to court, a marked shift began to emerge in her allegiance and that of her sons.

By mid-1595, Hugh O'Neill, the Earl of Tyrone, had shed all semblance of loyalty to the crown and had sent his brother, Art, to attack and capture the fort on the Blackwater, which Tyrone had earlier helped the English to build. It was a clear statement to the English that his previous protestations of loyalty were but a stalling tactic. A unique and formidable confederacy spearheaded by O'Neill and his less cautious ally, Red Hugh O'Donnell, was being shaped from out of the traditional whirlpool of Gaelic disunity. In their despatches to the Spanish court, O'Neill and O'Donnell now represented their cause for the first time as an 'Irish' one. They offered the 'crown of Ireland' to Philip, 'if he would deliver them from their English oppressors.'[14] But, as ever, personal vendettas and individual power struggles threatened the confederacy from the start. Nowhere else was this more blatantly apparent than in Mayo, where O'Donnell's aggression was to alienate Granuaile and her sons from the Ulster cause.

The O'Donnells of Tirconail had traditionally claimed overlordship of north Mayo — a claim that had ever been forcibly resisted by the Bourkes and their allies. To secure a passage into Connaught, Red Hugh O'Donnell sought to reactivate that claim. In June 1595, Sligo Castle, regarded as the key to the defence of Connaught, was captured and given to O'Donnell, affording him an unhindered passage into Mayo. To demonstrate the extent of his power to the as yet unaligned chieftains of Mayo, O'Donnell looted and plundered throughout the county. The Mayo chieftains were caught between two opposing forces and felt the brunt of both, as one observer reported:

> Through the fear the people have of Sir Richard Bingham, their necessity drives them to depend on O'Donnell, whom they hate for his pride and ambition and are weary of the burdens he daily lays upon them.[15]

However, Bingham's days as governor were numbered. A new conspiracy among his fellow administrators was afoot to remove him from Connaught. Fearing that the charges were stacked against him, Bingham fled to England in September and was promptly imprisoned. Sir Conyers Clifford was appointed governor in his place.

O'Donnell pushed home his advantage in Mayo, and the chieftains there had little option but to bow to his demands. Granuaile and Tibbot-ne-Long, despite the promises and submissions made to the queen, had little option but to align themselves with the Ulster chieftain and bear the harsh exactions he imposed. The new English governor, Sir Conyers Clifford, also sought their allegiance and met with Tibbot-ne-Long, who, displaying the calculation and cunning that were to stand him well over the coming traumatic years, played one side off against the other with commendable skill. The English in Connaught realised his worth. Because of the slaying in August of his half-brother, Edmund Bourke, as he attempted to escape from Galway gaol, Tibbot-ne-Long had emerged as the most powerful leader in the Bourke hierarchy. His power, particularly by sea, which because of the disturbed and desolate state of Mayo was regarded as an indispensable asset to both sides in the conflict, made him a formidable ally or foe. For Granuaile, the removal of Bingham was an answer to all that she had sought, and at the remarkable age of sixty-five years she returned to her career of 'maintenance' by sea.

In December 1595 an event occurred which was to shape

the future political direction taken by Granuaile and Tibbot-ne-Long. It centred, as it had for his father and generations of Bourkes before him, on the contentious and still seductive issue of the MacWilliamship. Rampant in Mayo, O'Donnell announced his intention of reviving the title outlawed by the English. In late December, all the Bourke septs of Mayo made their way to the ancient inaugural site at Rousakeera. O'Donnell arrived with an army, accompanied by many of his Ulster client chieftains. Blatantly and with great insensitivity, he physically excluded the Bourkes from their ancient ceremony and imposed his own MacWilliam on them, choosing Theobald, son of Walter Ciotach of Tirawley, the least eligible of the Bourke candidates. The selection was received with uproar by the Bourke septs. O'Donnell's hopes of Bourke allegiance against the English were decidedly weakened by his rashness and lack of judgment:

> Hitherto the old customs were the alternative to the Queen's government. Now, the choice was between the Queen's government and the old customs subject to the very heavy burden of O'Donnell's domination.[16]

To ensure that the other contenders for the MacWilliamship would not serve against him, O'Donnell took hostages with him back to Tirconail, including Tibbot-ne-Long. In the event, O'Donnell's MacWilliam failed to command the allegiance of most of the Bourke septs and was eventually driven out of Mayo.

With Bingham out of the picture, Granuaile busied herself again by sea. The lands of her son, out of which the queen had granted her maintenance, had been repeatedly ravaged by O'Donnell and his MacWilliam, and were once again desolate. She raided and plundered south and north. Her ships were reported operating off the coast of Thomond, where the Earl of Thomond was forced to do battle with some of her followers who had landed in search of plunder. In 1596 the Dean of Limerick, writing to the English council, reported that 'Grany ny Maly and Mac Neil of Barra invaded one anothers possessions though farre distant. . . .'[17] The fact that she was prepared and able to sail in a retaliatory mission to the Isle of Barra, off the coast of Scotland, is testimony to her great endurance. The sea took a heavy toll of life and health. Few seamen in the sixteenth century lived to such an advanced age. Fewer still could physically operate in such a demanding and dangerous environment, as she continued to do until the close of the century. Like most of her contemporaries she was powerless to avert the oncoming mayhem as every leader was sucked into the maw of the final futile struggle of Gaelic Ireland, led by O'Neill and O'Donnell, to win back lost ground and reinstate itself against the determined onslaught of England. Survival was now her single purpose.

The effects of O'Donnell's actions against the Bourkes did not take long to manifest themselves. On his escape from O'Donnell's custody, Tibbot-ne-Long returned to Mayo, now devastated by O'Donnell's raids. In February 1597, the English governor, Sir Conyers Clifford, took up duty in Connaught. His style of government differed greatly from Bingham's as he sought to attain the allegiance of the chieftains by conciliatory measures, rather than by force. He had already established friendship with Tibbot-ne-Long's brother-in-law, Donough O'Connor Sligo, at the English court. He immediately rewarded that friendship by recapturing Sligo Castle and reinstating O'Connor Sligo. Well satisfied with the outcome, O'Connor Sligo 'established friendship and concord between his brother-in-law, Theobald-ne-Long . . . and Sir Conyers Clifford.'[18] Tibbot-ne-Long, together with Richard Bourke, the Devil Hook's son, O'Malley, MacJordan and others agreed to terms with Clifford. They were pardoned of all past 'offences' and provided with cattle. In return, they agreed to pay the arrears of the Composition rent outstanding, support the governor and hand over pledges. Together with his new-found allies, Tibbot-ne-Long marched into Tirawley and as the *Annals of the Four Masters* recorded, 'expelled and banished MacWilliam . . . to O'Donnell. . . . The country generally on this occasion adhered to Tibóid-ne-Long and the Governor.'[19]

With most of Mayo siding with him, and the Ulster confederacy growing in strength, Tibbot-ne-Long fully realised his worth to the English, and put a price on his continuing loyalty. On 25 April 1597, he presented the governor with a set of fourteen demands for the continuation of his service against O'Donnell. Clifford sent the demands to the Privy Council for deliberation. The outcome was that Tibbot-ne-Long secured the lands of the MacWilliam and a title in consideration of the MacWilliamship. (The title was not granted until 1627 when Tibbot-ne-Long was created the first Viscount Mayo by Charles I.) He was granted the lands of those within his own sept who had been killed in rebellion. He received a company of foot soldiers in the queen's pay. He secured pardons for his half-brother, his ally, Richard Bourke, for whom he also secured a pension, his mother's half-brother, Dónal-na-Piopa, and others of his relations. To ensure his control over the septs of Mayo, he sought a commission to grant protections, a demand which was mitigated. The document served as a basis by which, over the coming years of upheaval and displacement, Tibbot-ne-Long emerged as the largest landowner in Mayo. His rise marked the decay of the Gaelic tribal system and the emergence of English civil law in Ireland.

From the English records which survive, it appears that Granuaile backed and profited from her son's arrangement with the English authorities. In August 1597 Clifford indicated to the lord deputy that he had 'given him [Tibbot-ne-Long], his mother and brother amongst them in money and other necessaries, £200',[20] for their services by sea.

Patriotism was not applicable to sixteenth-century Ireland. Granuaile's actions and those of her sons were guided by the struggle to survive. Physical survival against the power of the sea and the elements was undoubtedly Granuaile's first challenge. Survival by sea must have made the political obstacles she encountered during her lifetime seem insignificant by comparison. But the goal was the same. When her political strategy is examined within the context of her time, she emerges as a realist. Survival was the spur for any Gaelic leader either to resist the encroachment of individual English administrators, or to accept the changes to whatever degree would guarantee survival. The common enemy had not yet been identified and it was not until many decades later that words such as patriotism and nationalism became the spur for resistance and rebellion.

While opposing individual English administrators like Bingham when they impinged directly on her power, Granuaile ensured that she had friends in high places at critical times.

Although to the generations of historians who came after her the political manipulations of Granuaile might lack the obligatory patriotic gloss, the fact that her status as a political leader in Gaelic society was not diminished, but rather augmented, by her association with elements in the English administration, is sufficient proof of the appropriateness of her strategy.

As the revolt of the Ulster chieftains gathered momentum and spilled over into Mayo, the advantages won by Tibbot-ne-Long from the English took many years to materialise. O'Donnell and his MacWilliam repeatedly raided Mayo, giving those who opposed them little chance to recover. When, on 14 August 1598, the English were overwhelmed by the forces of O'Neill and O'Donnell at the Battle of the Yellow Ford, many of the Connaught chieftains who had stood aloof or who had aligned with the English governor, changed sides. Now virtually unopposed, O'Donnell raided at will through Mayo and Galway down to Thomond. In the autumn, he sent his MacWilliam and O'Doherty specifically to plunder Granuaile's territory around Murrisk and Burrishoole. The incident was enshrined in the line of a contemporary poem:

> *Gráinne na gCearbhach do creach*
>
> Grace of the Gamblers he plundered

It referred to her known ability at gambling with the gaming dice, although in this instance, with the political dice.

Now almost seventy, and in her declining years, Granuaile must surely have left her struggle with the sea and with the world in the capable hands of her sons. While their activities and the part they played in the concluding years of the century are well documented, there are few additional references to the activities of Granuaile. One of the final recorded notices of her appeared in the state papers in July 1601, in a despatch from the captain of an English warship. It is fittingly enough an account of his encounter with one of her galleys sailing on a mission of plunder:

> All the sails I have seen since I came upon the coast was a galley I met withal betwixt Teelin and Killibeggs, where I made her run on shore among the rocks, notwithstanding she rowed with thirty oars and had on board ready to defend her 100 good

shot, which entertained skirmish with my boat and had put her to the worst. But coming up with my ship to her rescue, I quickly with my great shot made an end to the fray. This galley comes out of Connaught and belongs to Grany O'Malley . . . this with one other galley was set out and manned with a people called the Flaherties who was proposed to do some spoils upon the countries and islands of MacSwyne Fanad and Mac-Swyne ne Doe about Lough Swilly and Sheephaven. . . .[21]

That Granuaile was still alive appears likely and, while not actively involved in this particular incident, it seems that under her direction her trade of 'maintenance by land and sea' was being continued by her followers.

Thus the extraordinary life of Granuaile ends as it begins — shrouded in uncertainty. The exact date of her death, as of her birth, is uncertain. From the evidence to hand, it appears that her death occurred at Carraigahowley Castle about 1603. She probably survived to hear of the defeat of O'Neill and O'Donnell at the battle of Kinsale, the final and conclusive milestone in the long and bloody struggle between the Gaelic world of her birth and the new world of her sons' adoption. Perhaps she also lived to hear of the death in March 1603 of Queen Elizabeth, her adversary and her benefactor. Tradition holds that she is buried in the ruins of the Cistercian abbey on Clare Island, an appropriate resting place for a Sea Queen.

While denied a place in the annals and histories of Ireland, Granuaile's memory remained alive among the people in the area where she once lived. The English also had good reason to remember her long after her death. Writing in 1623, the then English lord deputy, seeking to justify the seizure of fishing rights on the borders of Mayo and Galway, reminded the Privy Council, that the inhabitants of Mayo:

> have been always more apt to rebellion than any in that Kingdom, in soe much that the very women have borne armes there, whereof one Grany ne Maly was famous and is yett renowned by them. . . .[22]

In the west of Ireland her stone fortresses stand solidly still in remembrance of their audacious chatelaine. Her main abode, Carraigahowley, stands stark and brooding, the sea waves lapping gently at its stone walls. Across the bay on Clare Island the ruins of 'Grania's castle' evoke images of the Pirate Queen.

More recently, her story has fired the imagination in a wide range of creative disciplines, and her life has been depicted in fiction, music, dance, documentary and film. She has become the inspiration for women's self-awareness groups, both in Ireland and abroad, for yacht races and diving clubs named in her honour. A new interpretative centre depicting her life and times was opened by Her Excellency, Mary Robinson, President of Ireland, in Louisburgh on the shores of Clew Bay. Skilled craftsmen at Waterford Glass encapsulated the essence of her seafaring life in a unique study in the famed Irish crystal, for presentation to the people of Clare Island. The modern-day O'Malley clan, its members scattered throughout the world, have come together each year since 1953 to commemorate and celebrate their remarkable antecedent. The Granuaile Trust, founded by the clan, helps to develop projects in the cultural and environmental fields. Named in her honour, the newly built ferry, *The Pirate Queen*, brings visitors to Clare Island to view her castle and final resting place, while the Irish Lights vessel, *The Granuaile*, keeps a watching brief on the coasts once traversed by this intrepid seafarer.

But it is the swirls and flourishes on the parchment manuscripts of the sixteenth-century English state papers, the letters, despatches and memorabilia of the Tudor conquest of Ireland, that have preserved for posterity the tantalising character and career of Granuaile and the impact she made on that traumatic era. These relics, now brittle and faded with age, challenge our predisposed sense of convention, our assumptions regarding what is possible, and rip apart the shallow boundaries that society tends to impose on women — boundaries which Granuaile, by 'overstepping the part of womanhood', dared to breach. Above all, they allow us a glimpse of one of the greatest survivors of them all.

Opposite: *Above*: Her excellency Mary Robinson, President of Ireland, and author Anne Chambers at the opening of the Granuaile Visitor Centre, 1995. *Below*: Traditional Tomb of Granuaile, Clare Island Abbey (National Monuments Commission).

10

The Descendants of Granuaile

Granuaile left her struggle with the world in the capable hands of her two sons, Murrough-ne-Maor O'Flaherty and Tibbot-ne-Long Bourke. Both were to prove as able as their indomitable mother in the art of survival. Pragmatic and ambitious, both possessed the traits of compromise and cunning which, as the 1500s drew to their inevitably traumatic close, were the weapons essential to make it into the new century. Of similar outlook and character, they tended to operate in tandem and, as well as being blood-relations, they became close political allies. Although the older, Murrough-ne-Maor seemed content to be directed by his younger, more influential half-brother, and he lived to reap the rewards. Their lives are a unique commentary on a period of fundamental transition and change. Theirs is the story of the minor chieftains who, at the close of the sixteenth century, occupied the middle ground between the fixed battle-lines of two incompatible protagonists, trapped by events outside their control. Many became pawns in a momentous game of strategy. Others, like the sons of Granuaile, 'plotted their own moves and in a game within a game, became intrepid knights charting their own survival.'[1]

Initially it was their seapower and seafaring expertise, inherited from their mother, combined with the undoubted following they both enjoyed within their territories, that made them much sought after by the opposing sides. By August 1597, both were allied, ostensibly with the English governor against O'Donnell. However, in the last years leading up to Kinsale, as the balance of power shifted in Connaught between Clifford and O'Donnell, they flirted with both sides, to the utter consternation of the English administrators. 'I know not of one day's service that Tibbot-ne-Long hath performed,'[2] the machiavellian president of Munster, Sir George Carew, complained to the Privy Council. In 1599, a spy reported to the Earl of Essex:

> Tibbot-ne-Long was within with O'Donnell and O'Donnell did send out of him as pledges . . . the best of his country. Tyrone himself say they are agreed, but they will not have any know of it.[3]

There was one issue, however, guaranteed to make Tibbot-ne-Long act unambiguously. This was the vexing question of the MacWilliamship, which to the close of the century continued to be the divisive issue it had always been, and continued to arouse in him the emotive response that it had in his ancestors. Even when his ally, Clifford, was attacked and killed in the Battle of the Curlew mountains in 1599, it was the issue of the MacWilliamship that kept Tibbot-ne-Long from finally throwing in his lot with O'Donnell. The lands pertaining to the title — rather than the title itself — were now the magnet. As Tibbot-ne-Long well realised, the MacWilliamship would never again attain its original prestige, no matter which side emerged victorious in the coming confrontation. In his deal with the English, the Privy Council had conferred on him part of the MacWilliamship estate, and he had already moved with his family inland to Belcarra Castle. In 1600, on his return from a stint of dubious duty in Munster, leading an army in the queen's pay, he expelled O'Donnell's MacWilliam who, in his absence, had come into Mayo. Pressed by Sir Henry Docwra who had landed behind his lines in Lough Foyle, and by his rival, Nial Garv O'Donnell, Red Hugh O'Donnell could no longer support his MacWilliam. Now unopposed in Mayo, Tibbot-ne-Long convened a meeting of all the Bourke septs at Rousakeera, and conferred the MacWilliamship on his longtime ally, Granuaile's grandson, Richard Bourke, the son of the Devil's Hook.

To confer the MacWilliamship on a subordinate rather than assume the title himself was a shrewd move. Tibbot-ne-Long already possessed most of the lands and privileges once pertaining to the title. If he wished to maintain credence with the English, he could not be seen to assume a proscribed office.

Moreover, by conferring the title on a lesser chieftain, he demonstrated that he had, in effect, become greater than the once all-powerful MacWilliam. The final struggle for the ancient title in itself symbolised the final struggle being waged by the Gaelic world that had bred and sustained it through the centuries. Perhaps it was the inevitability of the decline of the MacWilliamship that made Tibbot-ne-Long refuse to be its last holder, preferring to be neither the holder of a doomed office, nor the champion of the doomed world that it represented.

On 23 September 1601, Spanish troops under the command of Don Juan del Aquila arrived to support the Ulster chieftains against the English. Inadvertently, they landed at Kinsale in the southernmost part of the country. The entire length of Ireland lay between them and O'Neill and O'Donnell in Ulster. In late October, the Spaniards were besieged by an army, ostensibly English but in reality composed of as many Irish, commanded by Lord Mountjoy. In Ulster, Red Hugh O'Donnell quickly mustered his army and, in an incredible feat of endurance, outmarched and outmanoeuvred the English forces sent to bar his way. At the end of November, his more cautious ally, Hugh O'Neill, also made the long journey south to Kinsale. With a combined army of 6,000, they besieged the besiegers. At the beginning of December, leading an army of 300, Tibbot-ne-Long marched out of Mayo and also headed south. As he approached Kinsale, neither Mountjoy nor O'Neill knew with certainty on which side he intended to fight. At Kinsale, after months of vacillation, Tibbot-ne-Long finally showed his hand and fought alongside the victorious Mountjoy.

Despite the defeat at Kinsale, at the beginning of the seventeenth century, the greater part of the land was still in Gaelic hands. A new war for possession of the land of Ireland commenced. With the collapse of the Gaelic system and the Flight of the Earls in 1607, vast areas were open to the lust for land of a new wave of English planters, adventurers and entrepreneurs, armed with vague and suspect titles to large properties. In this new war, waged with maps, quill and parchment, inquisitions and legal rhetoric, Tibbot-ne-Long's instinct for survival endured its greatest test. For the space of three decades

Extract of Letters Patent of knighthood, 1603 (Westport House mss).

he successfully competed within the framework of an alien legal system and increased his patrimony substantially, despite the crown's suspicions, and against the concerted efforts of the many foreign adventurers and speculators who sought to deny him. By mortgage, purchase, claim and counter-claim, by right both of Gaelic and English law, Tibbot-ne-Long amassed the largest estate in Mayo, mostly at the expense of his less well-off and legally astute relations, in particular the O'Malleys, various septs of the Bourkes and his foster family, the MacEvillys of Carra. After Kinsale he abandoned his seafaring activities to consolidate his position on land. The remains of his mother's fleet continued to be operated into the middle of the new century by Granuaile's O'Malley relations, but without her effectiveness or flamboyance.

Tibbot-ne-Long was knighted by the new king of England, James I, on 4 January 1603, in recognition of his 'loyal and valorous' service. He was styled Sir Tibbot (ne Longe) Bourke. The letters patent relating to his enoblement are preserved in Westport House. They are written in Latin on six pages of fine parchment and are hand coloured with the De Burgo arms, Tibbot-ne-Long's personal arms and a portrait of King James I. In 1627 he was created Viscount Mayo by Charles I. Despite his royal honours, however, the English never shed their suspicions about his loyalty. Until his death at Kinturk Castle in 1629, he continued to scheme and intrigue with exiled elements of the Gaelic resistance against whom he had fought at Kinsale, and endured imprisonment and investigation in the process. But being the survivor that he was, he managed to retain both his head and his newly acquired lands and titles, together with, paradoxically, the esteem and loyalty of his Gaelic followers and neighbours. He is buried in Ballintubber Abbey.

Murrough-ne-Maor predeceased his half-brother by three years. He died at Bunowen Castle in April 1626, and was buried, according to his wishes, in the Abbey of St Francis in Galway, the city from which his ancestors had once been debarred. In his will, by which he appointed Tibbot-ne-Long his executor, he provided for each of his eight sons and two daughters out of his large estate, which stretched from Bunowen north to Renvyle and south to Kilkieran. One of the stipulations of his will was the provision for

> my fifth son Patricke who is become a scholler, £20 when he is
> ready and determined to goe beyond the seas to studie, together
> with £10, everie year during his continuance beyond the seas.[4]

His eldest son, known as Murrough-ne-Mart (of the Beeves),
succeeded him and was knighted by the lord deputy, Sir Thomas Wentworth, in 1637. He was subsequently dispossessed of
his estates by the Cromwellian confiscations in 1653, and his
descendants who remained were gradually reduced to the
status of impoverished farmers.

The descendants of Granuaile through the marriage of her
daughter, Margaret O'Flaherty, to Richard Bourke, the Devil's
Hook, are unknown, as are also her O'Flaherty descendants
through her eldest son, Owen.

Tibbot-ne-Long's death notice was registered at Athlone
Castle. The entry reads:

> The right Honorable sr Theobald Burke Kt Viscount Burke of
> Mayo, deceased the 18 of June 1629. He had to wife Maude, dr
> of Charles O'Connor Sligoe, by whome he had issue, the right
> Ho. Miles, Viscount Burke, David, Theobald, Richard, Mary,
> Onora and Margaret. . . .[5]

His eldest son, Miles, perhaps named in honour of Tibbot-ne-
Long's foster father, Miles MacEvilly, whose lands and castles
of Kinturk, Kilboynell (afterwards Castlebourke) and Manulla
were by now subsumed into his estate, became the second
Viscount Mayo. Like his father, he endured the continuing
distrust of the English establishment, and for a time was
confined at the Gatehouse at Westminster. To hold onto his
estates, he outwardly conformed to the reformed religion. He
played a somewhat nefarious role in the massacre of Protestant settlers at Shrule in 1640. His son, Theobald, the third
viscount, who made a valiant attempt to avert the slaughter,
was subsequently tried, found guilty and executed by the
Cromwellians, more with an eye to his confiscated estates than
to his alleged involvement in the crime. Theobald, the fourth
viscount, was regranted only part of his estates on the restoration of Charles II. By the time of the last acknowledged
viscount, John Bourke, who died in 1767, the original Mayo
estate was reduced through confiscation and mortgage to

Castlebourke and a few hundred acres.

On the death of the eighth Viscount Mayo, who was considered to have no male heir, the title officially lay dormant. There is much evidence to suggest that it should not have been declared dormant but that on the death of the eighth viscount, the rightful claimant was a David Bourke from Asgalan in the barony of Murrisk — a direct descendant of Richard, the fourth son of Tibbot-ne-Long. His claim was supported by the depositions of the sister of the eighth viscount, the dowager countess of the seventh viscount and many of the retainers and friends of the last deceased viscount. To the doctor who attended him on his deathbed in 1790, David Bourke claimed to be the ninth Viscount Mayo. Richard Bourke, his uncle from Ballyhaunis, claimed as tenth viscount but had not the means to pursue his case through the courts. On his death, his son and heir, Michael Bourke of Lavalaroe, submitted additional sworn affidavits that he was 'the fourth cousin in the male line of collateral descent to the late John, lord Viscount Bourke of Mayo',[6] but because of his meagre means, his claim was not successful, and he died sometime after 1814. The Viscount Mayo title was subsequently subsumed into the Earldom of Mayo, a more recent creation.

Tibbot-ne-Long's Death Notice, 1629.

Maud Bourke (b. 1642), great-great granddaughter of Granuaile (Westport House).

The descendants of Granuaile are mainly traceable through her Bourke line, and her bloodline is to be found among many pedigrees of both aristocrat and commoner. Like Granuaile herself, some of her descendants made an impact on their age. Her great-great-great granddaughters were Maria and Elizabeth Gunning, known as the 'gorgeous Gunnings' from Castlecoote, Co. Roscommon. In the eighteenth century they took English society by storm with their beauty. One married the Earl of Coventry and subsequently the Duke of Hamilton; the other married the Duke of Argyle. In 1669, Granuaile's great-great-granddaughter, Maud Bourke, daughter of Theobald the third Viscount Mayo, married John Browne of Westport, whose mansion, Westport House, was built near the old O'Malley fortress of Cathair-na-Mart, where Dónal-na-Piopa, Granuaile's half-brother, once resided. Their descendants include Howe Peter Browne, Second Marquess of Sligo who, as governor

Westport House (Liam Lyons).

of Jamaica (1834–36) championed the emancipation of the slaves. The present owner of Westport House, Jeremy Browne, eleventh Marquess of Sligo, is thirteenth great-grandson in descent from Granuaile. Claiming a similar descent is the film producer, Lord John Brabourne, married to the daughter of the late Lord Louis Mountbatten. With tragic perversity, their son, Nicholas, a fourteenth great-grandson in descent from Granuaile, was killed with his grandfather, grandmother and young friend off Mullaghmore harbour in Sligo in 1979, in waters once traversed by his remarkable ancestor.

The descendants through Granuaile's O'Malley relations, particularly her half-brother, Dónal-na-Piopa, are less certain. Confiscation, deprivation and famine scattered the clan O'Malley throughout the world. The passage of time and lack of authentic records have rendered impossible the task of tracing individual O'Malley family branches back as far as the sixteenth century and unravelling their connections to Granuaile. But O'Malleys everywhere can take pride in the fact that they originate from the same seafaring clan from the lordship of Umhall on the west coast of Ireland, and that they share a common heritage with the most famous member of the clan to bear the name Ó Máille — Granuaile.

APPENDIX I

Poems and Songs

Granuaile

There stands a tower by the Atlantic side
A grey old tower, by storm and sea-waves beat
Perch'd on a cliff, beneath it yawneth wide
A lofty cavern of yore a fit retreat
For pirates galleys; altho', now, you'll meet
Nought but the seal and wild gull; from that cave
A hundred steps do upwards lead your feet
Unto a lonely chamber! — Bold and brave
Is he who climbs that stair, all slippery from the wave.

I sat there on an evening. In the west,
Amid the waters, sank the setting sun:
While clouds, like parting friends, about him prest,
Clad in their fleecy garbs, of gold and dun;
And silence was around me — save the hum,
Of the lone and wild bee, or the curlew's cry.
And lo! Upon me did a vision come,
Of her who built that tower, in days gone by;
And in that dream, behold! I saw a building high.

A stately hull — lofty and carved the roof —
Was deck'd with silken banners fair to see.
The hanging velvet, from Genou's woof,
And wrought with Tudor roses curiously;
At its far end did stand a canopy,
Shading a chair of state, on which was seen
A ladye fair, with look of majesty,
Amid a throng, 'yclad in costly sheen —
Nobles and gallant Knights proclaim her England's Queen.

The sage Elizabeth; and by her side
Were group'd her counsellors, with calm, grave air,
Burleigh and Walsingham, with others, tried
In wisdom and in war, and sparkling there,
Like Summer butterflies, were damsels fair,
Beautiful and young: behind a trusty band
Of stalwart yeomanry, with watchful care,
The portal guard, while nigher to its stand
Usher and page, ready to ape with willing hand.

A Tucket sounds, and lo! There enters now
A strange group, in saffron tunics drest:
A female at their head, whose step and brow
Herald her rank, and, calm and self possest,
Onward she came, alone through England's best,
With careless look, and bearing free yet high,
Tho' gentle dames their titterings scarce represt,
Noting her garments as she passed them by;
None laughed again who met that stern and flashing eye.

Restless and dark, its sharp and rapid look
Showd's a fierce spirit, prone a wrong to feel,
And quicker to revenge it. As a book.
That sun-burnt brow did fearless thoughts reveal;
And in her girdle was a skeyne of steel;
Her crimson mantle, a gold brooch did bind;
Her flowing garments reached unto her heel;
Her hair-part fell in tresses unconfined,
And part, a silver bodkin did fasten up behind.

'Twas not her garb that caught the gazer's eye —
Tho' strange, 'twas rich, and, after its fashion, good —
But the wild grandeur of her mien-erect and high.
Before the English Queen she dauntless stood,
And none her bearing there could scorn as rude;
She seemed as one well used to power — one that hath
Dominion over men of savage mood,
And dared the tempest in its midnight wrath,
And thro' opposing billows cleft her fearless path.

And courteous greeting Elizabeth then pays,
And bids her welcome to her English land
And humble hall. Each looked with curious gaze
Upon the other's face, and felt they stand
Before a spirit like their own. Her hand
The stranger raised — and pointing where all pale,
Thro' the high casement, came the sunlight bland,
Gilding the scene and group with rich avail;
Thus, to the English Sov'reign, spoke proud 'Grana Wale'.

Queen of the Saxons! From the distant west
I come; from Achill steep and Island Clare,
Where the wild eagle builds 'mid clouds, his nest,
And Ocean flings its billows in the air.
I come to greet you in your dwelling fair.
Led by your fame — lone sitting in my cave.
In sea — beat Donna — it hath reached me there,
Theme of the minstrel's song; and then I gave
My galley to the wind, and crossed the dark green wave.

'Health to thee, ladye!' — let your answer be
Health to our Irish land; for evil men
Do vex her sorely, and have buklar'd thee
Abettor of their deeds; lyeing train,
That cheat their mistress for the love of gain,
And wrong their trust — aught else I little reck,
Alike to me, the mountain and the glen —
The castle's rampart or the galley's deck;
But thou my country spare — your foot is on her neck.

Thus brief and bold, outspake that ladye stern,
And all stood silent thro' that crowded hall;
While proudly glared each proud and manly kern
Attendant on their mistress. Then courtly all
Elizabeth replies, and soothing fall
Her words, and pleasing to the Irish ear —
Fair promises — that she would soon recall
Her evil servants. Were these words sincere?
That promise kept? Let Erin answer with a tear!

O'Hart: *Irish Pedigrees*, vol. II, p. 675 (From the Irish)

Grana Weal

O thou that are sprung from the flow'r of the land,
Whose virtues endear and whose talents command;
When our foemen are banished, how then wilt thou feel
That the King of the right shall espouse Grana Weal.

O'er the high hills of Erin what bonfires shall blaze,
What libations be pour'd forth! — What festival days! —
What minstrels and monks with one heart-pulse of zeal,
Sing and pray for the King and his own Grana Weal!

The monarch of millions is riding the sea,
His revenge cannot sleep, and his guards will not flee;
No cloud shall the pride of our nobles conceal,
When the foes are dispersed that benight Grana Weal.

The mighty in thousands are pouring from Spain,
The Scots, the true Scots shall come back again;
To far-distant exile no more shall they steal,
But waft the right King to his fond Grana Weal.

Raise your hearts and exult, my beloved at my words,
Your eyes to your King, and your hand to your swords! —
The Highlands shall send forth the bonneted Gael,
To grace the glad nuptials of Grana Weal.

And Louis, and Charles and the heaven-guided Pope,
And the King of the Spaniards shall strengthen our hope;
One religion — one kindred — one soul shall they feel,
For our heart enthroned Exile and Grana Weal.

With weeping and wailing, and sorrow and shame —
And anguish of heart that no pity dare claim;
The craven English churls shall all powerless kneal
To the home-restored Stuart and Grana Weal.

Our halls will rejoice with friendship and cheer,
And our hearts be as free from reproach as from fear;
The hungry adventurer shall pine from the meal,
He long lapped from the life-stream of Grana Weal.

Ah! Knowest thou the maiden all beauteous and fair,
Whom her merciless foes have left plundered and bare?
The force of my emblem too well cant thou feel,
For that suffering lorn one is our Grana Weal.

But the nobles shall bring back the true king again
And justice long slighted will come in his train;
The bullets shall fly — and the cannons shall peal —
And our Charles victorious espouse Grana Weal.

James Hardiman: *Irish Minstrelsy*, vol. II, p. 65

Grace O'Malley

She left the close-air'd, land of trees,
And proud MacWilliam's palace,
For clear, bare Clare's health-salted breeze,
Her oarsmen and her galleys
And where, beside the bending strand
The rock and billow wrestle
Between the deep sea and the land
She built her island Castle

The Spanish captain, sailing by
For Newport, with amazement
Beheld the cannon'd longship lie
Moor'd to the lady's casement,
And, covering coin and cup of gold
In haste their hatches under,
They whisper'd "Tis a pirate's hold;
She sails the seas for plunder.'

But no: 'twas not for sordid spoil
Of barque or sea-board borough
She plough'd, with unfatiguing toil,
The fluent — rolling furrow;
Delighting, on the broad back'd deep,
To feel the quivering galley
Strain up the opposing hill, and sweep
Down the withdrawing valley:

Or, sped before a driving blast,
By following seas uplifted,
Catch, from the huge heaps heaving past,
And from the spray they drifted
And from the winds that toss'd the crest
Of each wide-shouldering giant,
The smack of freedom and the zest
Of rapturous life defiant.

For, oh the mainland time was pent
In close constraint and striving,
So many aims together bent
On winning and on thriving;
There was no room for generous case,
No sympathy for candour: —
And so she left Burke's buzzing trees,
And all his stony splendour.

For Erin yet had fields to spare
Where Clew her cincture gathers
Isle — gemmed; and kindly clans were there,
The fosterers of her fathers:
Room there for careless feet to roam
Secure from minions' peeping
For fearless mirth to find a home
And sympathetic weeping;

And generous ire and frank disdain
To speak the mind, nor ponder
How this in England, that in Spain,
Might suit to tell; as yonder,
Where daily on the slippery dais
By thwarting interests chequer'd
State gamesters played the social chess
Of politic Clanrickard.

Nor wanting quite the lovely isle
In civic life's adornings:
The Brehon's Court, might well beguile
A learned lady's mornings.
Quaint through the clamorous claim, and rude
The pleading that convy'd it,
Right conscience made the judgment good,
And loyal love obey'd it.

And music was sweeter far
For ears of native nurture,
Than virginals at Castlebar
To tinkling touch of courtier,
Where harpers good in hall struck up
The planxty's gay commotion,
Or, pipers scream'd from pennon'd poop
Their piobrach over ocean.

And sweet, to see, their ruddy bloom
Whom ocean's friendly distance
Preserved still unenslaved; for whom
No tasking if existence
Made this one rich and that one poor,
In gold's illusive treasure,
But all, of easy life secure,
Were rich in wealth of leisure.

Rich in the Muse's pensive hour,
In genial hour for neighbour,
Rich in young mankind's happy power
To live with little labour;
The wise, free way of life, indeed,
That still, with charm adaptive,
Reclaims and tames the alien greed,
And takes the conqueror captive.

Nor only life's unclouded looks
To compensate its rudeness;
Amends there were in holy books,
In offices of goodness,
In cares above the transient scene
Of little gains and honours,
That well repaid the Island Queen
Her loss of urban manners.

Sweet, when crimson sunsets glow'd,
As earth and sky grow grander,
Adown the grass'd, unechoing road
Atlantic ward to wander,
Some Kinsman's humbler hearth to seek,
Some sick-bed side, it may be,
Or, onward reach, with footsteps meek,
The low, grey, lovely, abbey:

And, where stories stone beneath
The guise of plant and creature,
Had fused the harder lines of faith
In easy forms of nature;
Such forms, on tell the master's pains
'Mong Roslin's carven glories,
Or hint the faith of Pictish' Thanes
On standing stones of Forres;

The Branch; the weird cherubic Beasts;
The Hart by hounds o'ertaken;
Or, intimating mystic feasts,
The self-resorbent Dragon; —
Mute symbols, though with power endow'd
For finer dogmas' teaching,
Than clerk might tell to carnal crowd
In homily or preaching; —

Sit; and while heaven's refulgent show
Grew airier and more tender,
And ocean gleaming floor below
Reflected loftier splendour,
Suffused with light, of lingering faith
And ritual lights reflection,
Discourse of birth, and life, and death,
And of the resurrection.

But chiefly sweet from morn to eve,
From eve to clear-eyed morning,
The presence of the felt reprieve,
From strangers' note and scorning:
No prying, proud, intrusive foes
To pity and offend her: —
Such was the life the lady chose,
Such choosing, we commend her.

                              Sir Samuel Ferguson.

The following song originated in Co. Leitrim around Ballinamuck and it is thought that it originated about 1798 with the survivors from Mayo of the Battle at Ballinamuck between the Franco-Irish forces and the English.

Granuaile

As the sunlight in its glory
Ever shines on fair Clew Bay
And Croagh Patrick old and hoary
Rises o'er the ruins grey
As the streamlets in the meadows
In their pride come dancing down
Nestled close among the mountains
Stands pleasant Newport Town.

Just a mile from where the turrets
Of the ancient town uprise
And the frowning peak of Nephin
Soars in grandeur to the skies
Lie a massive heap of ruins
In their loneliness sublime
Though scattered and dismantled now
By tyranny and time

'Twas a proud and stately castle
In the years of long ago
When the dauntless Grace O'Malley
Ruled a queen in fair Mayo.
And from Bernham's lofty summit
To the waves of Galway Bay
And from Castlebar to Ballintra
Her unconquered flag held sway.

She had strongholds on her headlands
And brave galleys on the sea
And no warlike chief or viking
E'er had bolder heart than she.
She unfurled her country's banner
High o'er battlement and mast
And 'gainst all the might of England
Kept it flying 'til the last.

The armies of Elizabeth
Invaded her on land
Her warships followed on her track
And watched by many a stand
But she swept her foes before her
On the land and on the sea
And the flag of Grace O'Malley
Waved defiant, proud and free.

On the walls of Carrick Clooney
As the Summer sun went down
And its last bright rays were fading
On the spires of Newport town.
To the watchmen on the ramparts
There appeared in long array
A band of English spearmen
By the waters of Clew Bay.

To the walls flew Grace O'Malley
With her clansmen at her side
Who had often met the foemen
On the land and on the tide.
But she saw the marshalled strength
Of the English coming on
And the colour of their armour
That in polished brightness shone.

Soon before the frowning battlements
The English columns came
Whilst on the walls before them
Stood many a bristling gun.
Then forwards towards the barbican
A herald quickly came
And demanded free admittance
In the English monarch's name.

He said 'My Royal Mistress
Sends her men-at-arms and me
With greetings good to all her friends
Who true and loyal be.
Her liegeman, Lord Hal Sydney
With all his spears awaits
For you to open wide to him
The Barbican and gates!

'So tell your Royal mistress,'
The dauntless Grace replied,
'That she and all her men-at-arms
Are scornfully defied.
She may own the fertile valley
Where the Foyle and Liffey flow
But tell her Grace O'Malley
Is unconquered in Mayo.'

'Our flag upon the battlements
Is to the breeze outthrown
And with God's grace we'll keep it there
In spite of Queen and throne.
There's many a brave O'Malley here
With me to man the walls
And rally round the flag we love
Until the last man falls!

'We want no English hirelings here
No soldiers of the Crown
We falter not before their spears
Nor cower beneath their frown.
No! Clansmen, let your warcry ring
Defiance on the gale
And greet those braggart Saxons
With a shower of Irish hail.'

Then sprang upon the Britons
With many a loud hurrah
A band of fierce and rugged men
Well brazed in many a fray.
On every tower and battlement
The Irish kern appears
And fiercely flash their guns upon
The foe's advancing spears.

The dauntless Grace with Spartan soul
Stands on the outer wall.
Regardless of the shower of balls
That fast around them fall.
The English come with marshalled strength
And nerved with deadly hate
They fiercely clash through friends and foes
And gain the foremost gate.

But right before them face to face
The clansmen of Mayo
Start up and greet those robbers well
With thrust and sabre blow.
And rushing fierce as mountain stream
Through dark and flooded glen
Leaps to the gate, the dauntless Grace
And all her fearless men.

Hurrah! Their spears are backward borne
Their blood-red flag is down
And Sydney vanquished and pursued
Spurs hard to Newport Town.
This lesson taught the Saxon churl
To dread a Free-man's blow
When the dauntless Grace O'Malley
Ruled a Queen in fair Mayo.

The walls of Carrick Clooney
Now lie crumbling and low
Its battlements dismantled are
All moss o'er every stone.
But the rebel youth in Westport
Feel their Irish hearts aglow
When they tell how Grace O'Malley
Fought and conquered in Mayo.

There's many a fearless rebel
In Westport and Clew Bay
Who watch with longing eagerness
For Freedom's dawning day.
There's many a brawny mountaineer
Prepared to strike a blow
For the old Green Flag and Freedom
On the soil of brave Mayo.

James Hardiman: Irish Minstrelsy, vol. II

Oró, Sé do Bheatha 'bhaile

I

Sé do bheatha! a bhean ba leanmhar!
B'é ár gceach tú bheith i ngéibhinn,
Do dhuiche bhrea i seilbh meirleach
'S tú diolta leis na Gallaibh.

Oró! Sé do bheatha 'bhaile!
Oró! Sé do bheatha 'bhaile!
Oró! Sé do bheatha 'bhaile!
Anois ar theacht an tSamhraidh.

II

Tá Gráinne Mhaol ag teacht thar sáile,
Óglaigh armtha lei mar gharda;
Gaeil iad féin 's ní Gaill ná Spainnigh
'S cuirfid ruaig ar Ghallaibh.

III

A bhuí le Rí na bhfeart go bhfeiceam,
Muna mbeam beo 'na dhiaidh ach seachtain,
Gráinne Mhaol agus mile gaiscíoch
Ag fógairt fáin ar Ghallaibh.

Pádraig Mac Phiarais

Oró and Welcome Home

I

Welcome, O woman who was sorrowful
We were desolate while you were imprisoned.
Your lovely country in the hands of vandals
And you yourself — sold to the English.

Chorus:

Oró — and welcome home,
Oró — and welcome home,
Oró — and welcome home,
Would that the Summer is here.

II

Gráinne Mhaol is coming over the sea,
With a guard of young soldiers,
They are Irish, not English or Spanish
And they will rout the English.

III

Thanks be to God that I'm seeing
(Even If I only live for a week after!)
Gráinne Mhaol and a thousand warriors
Announcing ruin on the English.

Pádraig Pearse (translated)

Granuweal — An old song

I

A courtier call'd Dorset, from Parkgate did fail,
In his Majesty's yacht, for to court Granuweal;
With great entertainment the thought to prevail,
And rifle the charms of Granuweal.

Chorus:

Sing Budderoo, didderoo, Granuweal,
The Fox in the Trap we have caught by the tail
Sing success to the sons of brave Granuweal.

II

Says the courtier to Granu, if you will be true,
I will bring you to London, and do for you too;
Where you shall have pleasure that never will fail,
I'll laurel your Shamrock, sweet Granuweal.

III

Says Granu to Dorset, if that I would do,
Bring my fortune to London, my children would rue;
We would be like Highlanders eating of keal,
And cursing the union, says Granuweal.

IV

Says Granu, I always was true to my king;
When in war, I supply'd him with money and men.
Our love to King George with our blood we did seal,
At Dettingen battle, says Granuweal.

V

Says Granu, I always still lov'd to be free;
No foe shall invade me in my liberty.
While I've Limerick, Derry and the fort of Kinsale,
I'll love and not marry, says Granuweal.

VI

Says Granu, you see there's a large stone put in,
To the heart of the church, by the leave of the King.
The works of this stone shall be weigh'd in a scale,
With balance of justice, says Granuweal.

VII

I hope our brave Harrington, likewise Kildare,
Our trade and our commerce once more will repair,
Our lives we will venture with greatest affail,
Against French and Spaniards, says Granuweal.

VIII

Now, my dear boys, we've got shut of those bugs,
I charge you my children, lie close in your rugs,
They'll hide like a snake, but will bite I'll be bail,
I'll give them shillelagh, says Granuweal.

Poor Old Granuaile

My dream to some with joy will come and comes with grief to
    more,
As it did to me, my country, that dear old Erin's shore;
I dreamt I stood upon a hill beside a lovely vale,
And it's there I spied a comely maid and her name was
    Granuaile.

Her lovely hair hung down so fair and she was dressed in green,
I thought she was the fairest soul that e'er my eyes had seen;
As I drew near I then could hear by the pleasant morning gale,
As she went along she sang her song saying 'I'm poor old
Granuaile'.

In O'Connell's time in '29 we had no braver men,
They struggled hard both day and night to gain our rights again;
Still, by coercion we were bound and our sons were sent to jail,
'You need not fret, we'll Home Rule get,' says poor old Granuaile.

I thought she had a splendid harp by her side she let it fall,
She played the tunes called Brian Boru, Garryowen, and Tara's
Hall.
Then God Save Ireland was the next, and Our Martyrs Who
Died in Jail,
'You need not fret, we'll have freedom yet,' says poor old
Granuaile.

When I wakened from my slumber and excited by my fight,
I thought it was the clear daylight, and I found that it was night;
I looked all round and could see naught but the walls of a
lonely jail.
And that was the last I ever saw of poor old Granuaile.

Irish Street Ballads collected and annotated by
Colm Ó Loughlainn, London 1928

A New Song Called Granuaile

All through the north as I walked forth to view the shamrock
plain
I stood a while where nature smiled amid the rocks and
streams
On a matron mild I fixed my eyes beneath a fertile vale
As she sang her song it was on the wrongs of poor old
Granuaile

Her head was bare and her grey hair over her eyes hung down
Her waist and neck, her hands and feet, with iron chains were
bound
Her pensive strain and plaintive wail mingled with the evening
gale
And the song she sung with mournful tongue was Poor Old
Granuaile.

The gown she wore was stained with gore all by a ruffian band
Her lips so sweet the monarchs kissed are now grown pale
and wan
The tears of grief fell from her eyes each tear as large as hail
None could express the deep distress of poor old Granuaile.

On her harp she leaned and thus exclaimed 'My royal Brian is
gone
Who in his day did drive away the tyrants every one
On Clontarf's plains against the Danes his faction did prepare.
Brave Brian Boru cut their lines in two and freed old Granuaile.

'But now, alas, I must confess, avengers I have none
There's no brave Lord to wave his sword in my defence — not
one
My enemies just when they please with blows they do assail
The flesh they tore clean off the bones of poor old Granuaile.

Six hundred years the briny tears have flowed down from my
eyes
I curse the day that Henry made of me proud Albion's prize
From that day down with chains I'm bound no wonder I look
pale
The blood they drained from every vein of poor old Granuaile.'

There was a lord came from the south he wore a laurel crown
Saying 'Grania dear, be of good cheer, no longer you'll be
bound
I am the man they call great Dan, who never yet did fail
I have got the bill for to fulfil your wishes Granuaile.'

With blood besmeared and bathed in tears her harp she
sweetly strung
And oh the change, her mournful air from one last chord she
wrung
Her voice so clear fell on my ear, at length my strength did fail
I went away and thus did say, 'God help you, Granuaile'.

The Family Connections of
GRACE O'MALLEY
(b. 1530 d. 1603 c.)

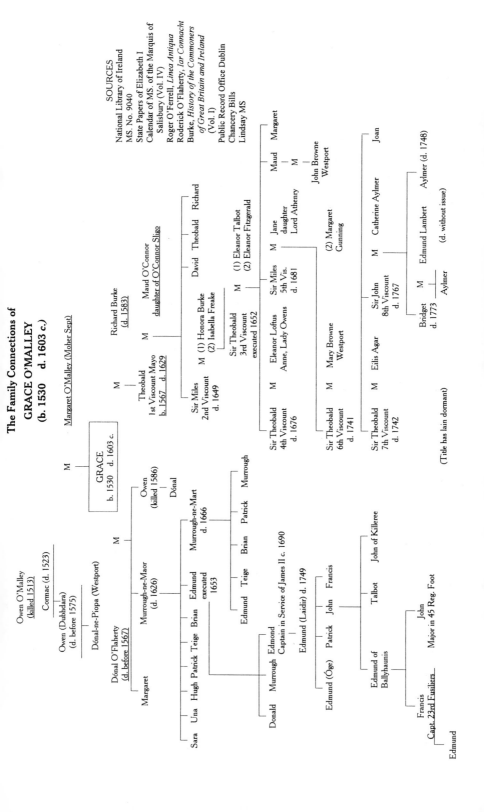

SOURCES
National Library of Ireland
MS. No. 9040
State Papers of Elizabeth I
Calendar of MS. of the Marquis of
Salisbury (Vol. IV)
Roger O'Ferrell, *Linea Antiqua*
Roderick O'Flaherty, *Iar Connacht*
Burke, *History of the Commoners
of Great Britain and Ireland*
(Vol. I)
Public Record Office Dublin
Chancery Bills
Lindsay MS

Owen O'Malley
(killed 1513)

Cormac (d. 1523)

Owen (Dubhdara)
(d. before 1575)

Dónal-ne-Piopa (Westport)

Margaret O'Malley (Moher Sept)

M

GRACE
b. 1530 d. 1603 c.

Dónal O'Flaherty
(d. before 1567)

M

Murrough-ne-Maor
(d. 1626)

Richard Burke
(d. 1583)

M

Theobald
1st Viscount Mayo
b. 1567 d. 1629

Maud O'Connor
daughter of O'Connor Sligo

Margaret Una Hugh Patrick Teige Brian Edmund
executed
1653

Owen
(killed 1586)

Dónal

Murrough-ne-Mart
d. 1666

Sara

Edmund Teige Brian Patrick Murrough

Donald Murrough Edmond
Captain in Service of James II c. 1690

Edmund (Laidir) d. 1749

Edmund (Óge) Patrick John Francis

Edmund of
Ballyhaunis

Talbot John of Killeree

Francis
Capt. 23rd Fusiliers

John
Major in 45 Reg. Foot

Edmund

Sir Miles
2nd Viscount
d. 1649

M (1) Honora Burke
(2) Isabella Freake

David Theobald Richard

Sir Theobald
3rd Viscount
executed 1652

M (1) Eleanor Talbot
(2) Eleanor Fitzgerald

Sir Theobald
4th Viscount
d. 1676

M Eleanor Loftus
Anne, Lady Owens

Sir Miles
5th Vis.
d. 1681

M Jane
daughter
Lord Athenry

Maud Margaret

M

John Browne
Westport

Sir Theobald
6th Viscount
d. 1741

M Mary Browne
Westport

(2) Margaret
Gunning

Sir Theobald
7th Viscount
d. 1742

M Eilis Agar

Sir John
8th Viscount
d. 1767

M Catherine Aylmer

Joan

Bridget
d. 1773

M

Aylmer

Edmund Lambert Aylmer (d. 1748)

(d. without issue)

(Title has lain dormant)

Descendants of Maud Bourke and John Browne

APPENDIX III

Granuaile's Petition to Queen Elizabeth I, July 1593

To the Queen's Most Excellent Majesty

In most humble Wise showeth unto your most excellent Majestie your loyall and faitefull subject Grany ny Mally of Conaght in your highnes realme of Ireland:– that wheras by meanes of the continnuall discord stirres and dissention that heretofore long tyme remained among the Irishrye especially in West Conaght by the sea side every cheeftaine for his safegard and maintenance and for the defence of his people followers and countrye took armes by strong hand to make head against his neyborhes which in like manner constrained your highnes fond subject to take armes and by force to maintaine her selfe and her people by sea and land the space of fortye yeares past. During which tyme she married Offlahertye being natural mother of his lawfull sone and heire nowe living and after his death married Mac William the cheefe of the Bourkes of West Conaght who died X yeares past, since which tyme she remaineth widowe and is likewise the mother of his lawfull sone and heyre nowe living. The countryes and teritories of which cheeftaines after the rude custome of their ancestores never yeilded doweries or thirds to the ladies thereof, and the rents services and reservation of the same was not certayne but confused the people for yelding to the cheeftaines whatever they would crave more than of ryght they aught to have. And now whereas by your gracious meanes the said province is reduced to that civill course that the cheeftaines freeholders or gents. hath compounded and is assigned what and how much he is to have; in which composition no order was taken for your fond subject what maintenance she aught to have of her former husbands lands and by the same is restrayned to use her former course to her utter decay and ruine: In tender consideracon wherof and in regard of her great age she most humbly besechethe your Majestie of your princely bounty and liberaltye to grant her some resonable maintenance for the little tyme she hath to lyve. And wheras your said subjects two sones are the lawfull heyres of the lands of there foresaid fathers wherof they nowe stand seized and possessed, that it would please your Royall Majestie to direct your gracious letters to your L. Deputy of your said realme willing him to accept a surrender at her hands of her said sones yelding to Your Majestie your heyrs and successors such yearly rents as conventiently such lands may yeld and they to hold the same by letters patents to them and ther heyres for ever and to grant the like for the lands of Walter Burgh Fitz Theobald Reogh and Shane Burke Mac William Mac Moiler cosen germaine to her said son. And lastly that it would please your Majestie to grant unto your said subject under your most gracious hand of signet free libertye during her lyve to envade with sword and fire all your highnes enemyes whersoever they ar or shal be without any interruption of any person or persons whatsoever. Thus shall your said subject according to her bounden duty ever remayne in all obedient alleagance to resist all remnants of rebellious enemies and pray continually for your Majesties long life and prosperous reygne.

Source: State Papers Elizabeth I.

Deciphered from the original by author.

APPENDIX IV

The Petition of Grany ny Mally to the Lord Treasurer, 5 May 1595

To the right honorable and my very good lord high treasurer of England.

Right Honorable and my very good lo. maye it hath pleased her Matie. At my last beinge here by her highness letters to Sr Richard Bingham to demand hime to take present order that I might possess and injoie the third parte of the lands and comodities of Mc William and O'Flahertie as lawful wif unto each of them so it is right honorable that I cane not have nor can injoie the same by meenes of Sir Richard Binghams hard dealing. I therefore most humblie beseeche your honours to be a meynes to her Matie to addres mye her highnes letters to the lo. Deputie to put me in the possession of the third parte of the said McWilliam and O'Flahertie my late husbands land and lyvinge and that likewise I maye lyve secure of my life which hath been atempted sundrie tymes to be said Sr Richard Bingham his brethern and others by his direcsion, humbly I beg your Treas.'s favourable letters in my owne and me sonnes behalf to the lo Deputie and to Sr Richard Bingham so cravinge pardon for my contynuall boldness . . . the livinge God to blesse and preserve yor Lord.

Source: State Papers Elizabeth I.

Deciphered from the original by author.

Appendix V

Signed Letter by Theobald Bourke — Tibóid-ne-Long (Toby of the Ships), to Anthony Brabazon, English Commissioner of Connaught

I have received your Honors letters and according as I have formerly written that I should be advertised of the meeting doiet eight daies before the appointeing thereof: I have not received the said advertisement but the eight of this month wheras you would have me to meete the IX of this month. Wherfore I desire yor. Honor to forbeare till the eighteen of this month and in the meane time, wee will prepare our complaints and agrievances and will be provided with provisions and other necessaries wch cannot be done before that time. As for Odonelle I perceive by his letters that he is likewise to answeare in that case for others in Connought and do here he will be ther the daie before menconed. Further for as much as Gallaway men do not furnishe us with anie commodities wee desire yor. Honor to direct yor. warrant unto the Mayor to th'end that we maye be furnished with such things as ys expedient excepting munitions for warres and with all to send a provision for those as will repaire for things to Gallawaye. Thus desiring yor. Honor to do not faile therin. I bide yo hartely farewell. ffrom camp the VIIIth of June 1596.

Signed Theobald Bourk

Source: State Papers Elizabeth I.

Deciphered from the original by author.

APPENDIX VI

The Eighteen
'Articles of Interrogatory'

TO BE ANSWERED BY GRANY NIMALY

1. Who was her father and mother
2. Who was her first husband
3. What sons she had by him. What be their names and where they live
4. What countries they have to maintain them withal
5. To whom they be married
6. What kin was O'Flaherty her first husband to Sir Mourrough M'Ne Dough O'Flaherty that is here now at the court
7. To answer the like question for her 2 husband and for his sons and their livings.
8. If she were to be allowed her dower, or thirds of her husbands living of what value the same might be of
9. Where upon the Composition of Connaught there hath been any provisions for the wives.
10. Whether it be not against the Customs of Ireland for the wives to have more after the deaths of their husbands than they brought with them
11. How she hath had maintenance and living since her last husband's death?
12. Of what kindred is Walter Bourgh fitz Tibalds and Shane Bourke mc Moyler to her son
13. What captains and countries lie next to her first husband's possessions
14. Who doth possess the house of Moriske upon the seaside in Owle O'Maly

15. What lands doth McGibbon possess in that country

16. Who doth possess the country named Carramore and Mayn Connell

17. Who doth possess the island of Achill and Kill castle

18. What kin was her last husband to Walter and Ulick Bourke

ANSWERS OF GRANY NY MALLY TO THE ARTICLES

To the first

Her father was called Doodarro O Mailly sometime chieftain of the country called Opper Owle O Mailly now called the barony of Murasky her mother was called Margaret ny Mailly daughter to Conogher Omailly of the same country and family. The whole country of Owle O Mailly aforesaid have these islands viz. Inish Boffyny Cleria Inish Twirke Inish arke Caher Inishdalluff Davellen and other small islands of little value which and the rest of the mainland are divided into the towns to the number of twenty and to every town four quarters or ploughs of land is assigned; out of every such quarter of land is yearly paid to her Majesty ten shillings called the composition rent. There is also in Connaught a country called Owle Eighter, otherwise the Lower or Nether Owle, containing fifty towns at four quarters the town, yearly paying the same rent, whereof the Sept of the Mailles in general hath twenty towns, the Bourkes of Mac William country other twenty towns and the Earl of Ormond ten towns.

To the second

Her first husband was called Donell Ichoggy Offlaherty and during his life chieftain of the Barony of Ballynehenssy, containing twenty-four towns at four quarters of land to every town paying yearly the composition rent aforesaid. After his death Teige Offlaherty the eldest son of Sir Morough now at court entered into Ballynehenssy afore said there did build a strong castle and the same with the demain lands thereof kept many years. Which Teige in the last rebellion of his father was slain.

To the third

She had two sons by her said first husband the eldest called Owen Offlahertie married Katherin Bourke daughter of Edmond Bourke of Castle Barry by her he had a son named Donell Offlahertie, now living which Owen all his lifetime remained a true subject to Her Majesty under the government of Sir Nicholas Malby while he lived and under Sir Richard Bingham until July 1586 at which time the Bourkes of the McWilliams country and the sept of the Shoose[Joyce] began to rebel. The said Owen, according to Sir Richards special direction, did withdraw himself his followers and tenants, with all their goods and cattle into a strong island for their more and better assurance. Then having been sent against the said rebels five hundred soldiers under the leading of Captain John Bingham appointed by his brother Sir Richard Bingham as the lieutenant in those parts. When they missed both the rebels and their cattle they came to the mainland right against the said island calling for victualls; whereupon the said Owen came forth with a number of boats and ferried all the soldiers into the island where they were entertained with the best cheer they had. That night the said Owen was apprehended and tied with a rope with eighteen of his chief followers; in the morning the soldiers drew out of the island four thousand cows, five hundred stud mares and horses and a thousand sheep leaving the remainder of the poor men all naked within the island [they] came with the cattle and prisoners to Ballynehenssy afor said where John Bingham afor said stayed for their coming; that evening he caused the said eighteen persons without trial or good cause to be hanged among whom was hanged a gentleman of land and living called Thebault O Twohill being of the age of four score and ten years. The next night following a false alarm was raised in the camp in the dead of the night the said Owen being fast bound in the cabin of Captain Grene O Mulloy and at that instant the said Owen was cruelly murdered having twelve deadly wounds and in that miserable sort he ended his years and unfortunate days — Captain William Mostyn now at court and Captain Merriman and Captain Mordant were of that company. Her second son called Moroghe Offlahertie now living is married to Honora Bourke daughter to Richard Bourke of Derivillaghny in the Magheri Reagh within the county of Galway.

To the fourth

Moroghe her second son aforesaid and Donell son to her first son the aforesaid Owen murdered do possess and enjoy the fourth part of the Barony of Ballynehenssy aforesaid unto them descended from their ancestors which is all the maintenance they have.

To the fifth
This is answered more at large to the third article.

To the sixth
Her first husband by the mother's side of Sir Moroghe now at court was his cousin germain and also cousins both being descended of one stock and root of nine degrees of consanguinity asunder.

To the seventh
Her second husband was called Sir Richard Bourke Knight alias McWilliam chief of the Bourkes of Nether or Low Connaught by him she had a son called Theobald Bourke now living he is married to Mewffe O'Connor sister to O'Connor Sligo now at court, his inheritance is about 40 quarters of land situated in the three baronies of Carry [Carra], Nether Owle and Galling [Gallen].

To the eighth
The countries of Connaught among the Irishry never yielded any thirds to any woman surviving the chieftain whose rent was uncertain for the most part extorted but now made certain by the composition and all Irish exactions merely abolished.

To the ninth
The Composition provided nothing to relieve the wife of any chieftain after his death wherin no mention is made of any such.

To the tenth
Among the Irishry the custom is that wives shall have but her first dowry without any increase or allowance for the same time out of mind it hath been so used and before any woman do deliver up her marriage portion to her husband she receives sureties for the restitution of the same in manner and form as she hath delivered it in regard that husbands through their great expenses especially chieftains at the time of their deaths have no goods to leave behind them but are commonly indebted; at other times they are divorced upon proof of precontracts; and

the husband now and then without any lawful or due proceeding do put his wife from him and so bringeth in another; so as the wife is to have sureties for her dowry for fear of the worse.

To the eleventh

After the death of her last husband she gathered together all her own followers and with 1,000 head of cows and mares departed and became a dweller in Carrikahowlly in Borisowle parcel of the Earl of Ormond's lands in Connaught and in the year 1586 after the murdering of her son Owen the rebellion being then in Connaught Sir Richard Bingham granted her his letters of tuition against all men and wiled her to remove from her late dwelling at Borisowle and to come and dwell under him, in her journey as she travelled was encountered by the five bands of soldiers under the leading of John Bingham and thereupon she was apprehended and tied in a rope, both she and her followers at that instant were spoiled of their said cattle and of all that ever they had besides the same and brought to Sir Richard who caused a new pair of gallows to be made for her last funeral where she thought to end her days, she was let at liberty upon the hostage and pledge of one Richard Bourke otherwise called the Devil's Hook when he did rebel fear compelled her to fly by sea into Ulster and there with O'Neill and O'Donnell staid three months; her galleys by a tempest being broken. She returned to Connaught and in Dublin received her Majesty's pardon by Sir John Perrot six years past and so made free. Ever since she dwelleth in Connaught a farmers life very poor bearing cess and paying Her Majesty's composition rent, utterly did she give over her former trade of maintenance by sea and land.

To the twelfth

Walter Bourke FitzThebalt and Shane Bourke FitzMeiller are cousins germain removed of one side viz. Walter son to Thebault, son to Meiller son to the said Walter Faddy. Thebault Bourke mentioned in the seventh article and born by Grany Ny Mailly son to Sir Richard Bourke her last husband, which Sir Richard was brother to the said Walter Faddy.

To the thirteenth

The country of her first husband is situated between Owle O'Mailley on the north west part, Mac William's country to the north east towards the country of Sligo, Sir Moroghe Offlaherties country on the east side towards Galway and the great bay of Galway on the south.

To the fourteenth

The castle town and lands of Morrisky is possessed by Owen M'Thomas O'Mailley now chieftain by the name of O'Mailley.

To the fifteenth

The Mac Gibbons have no lands by inheritance in any part of the country; farmers they are at will both to the Bourkes and to the O'Maillies.

To the sixteenth

She doth not know or understand Caremore or Moinconnell.

To the seventeenth

The island of Ackill is occupied by some of the Mailleys as tenants to the Earl of Ormond, as for Kill castle, she knoweth no town of that name.

To the eighteenth

Her last husband had two brothers Walter and Ulligge [Ulick] Bourke both died before she married Sir Richard Bourke, her said husband, their father was called David Bourke.

A set of 18 questions by Lord Burghley, the Lord Treasurer of England, dated July 1593, with appropriate answers by Granuaile.

Source: State Papers, Elizabeth I.

Deciphered from the original by the author.

References

Chapter 1: Powerful by Land and Sea

1. MS 1440, TCD.
2. Ordnance Survey Letters, Mayo, vol. II, p. 97.
3. *The Stranger in Ireland*, p. 304.
4. *A Chorographical Description of West Connaught*, p. 140.
5. *Ibid.*
6. *History of the County Mayo*, p. 189.
7. *Revue Celtique*, vol. XLIX, p. 174.
8. *Annals of the Four Masters*, vol. II, p. 1019.
9. *Ibid.* vol. 4, p. 815.
10. *Revue Celtique*, vol. XLIX, p. 175.
11. *History of the Town and County of Galway*, p. 83.
12. *Ibid.* p. 64.
13. *Ibid.* p. 201.
14. *Annals of Ulster*, vol. 3, p. 69.
15. SPI 63/19/56.
16. *Bold in Her Breeches*, p. 21.
17. Calendar of State Papers (Elizabeth I), vol. CCVI, p. 335.
18. *Ibid.* vol. CCVI, p. 335.
19. Lord of the Isles Voyage Brochure.
20. Calendar State Papers (Elizabeth I), vol. CCVI, p. 89.
21. Calendar of State Papers (Elizabeth I), vol. CCVI, p. 335.

Chapter 2: The World of Granuaile

1. Ordnance Survey Letters, Mayo, vol. II.
2. The Discourses, Book III, ch. 26.
3. Discourse of Ireland, p. 357.
4. Chancery Bill, no. R. 63.
5. Calendar State Papers (Edward VI), vol. CLXX, p. 132.
6. *Beginnings of Modern Ireland*, p. 30.
7. *A Chorographical Description of West Connaught*, p. 58.
8. Royal Irish Academy, MS no AV2, Folio 53A.

9. *The Buccaneer Queen*, p. 24.
10. *Irish Life in the 17th Century*, p. 338.
11. *Social History of Ancient Ireland*, p. 284.
12. *Ibid.*
13. *A Chorographical Description of West Connaught*, p. 383.

Chapter 3: Fortuna Favet Fortibus

1. *Irish Life in the 17th Century*, p. 338.
2. Ordnance Survey Letters, Mayo, vol. II, p. 97.
3. SPI 63/170/63.
4. *Ibid.*
5. Calendar State Papers (Elizabeth I), vol. CCVII, p. 5.
6. Dept. Celtic Studies, ms. no. 532.
7. *A Chorographical Description of West Connaught*, p. 385.
8. SPI 63/170/63.
9 *Ibid.*
10. SPI 63/170/19.

Chapter 4: The Pirate Queen

1. SPI 63/170/204.
2. SPI 63/171/18.
3. Lambeth Palace Library, ms. no. 601, p.111.
4. Calendar State Papers (James I) 1623, no. 997.
5. Ordnance Survey Letters, Mayo, vol. II.
6. Dept Celtic Studies, Folklore Collection, ms. no. 1134.
7. *The Way That I Went*, p. 184.
8. *Great Book of Genealogies*, p. 3259.
9. Gaisford St Lawrence Papers.
10. *Howth and its Owners*, p 182.
11. Ordnance Survey Letters, Mayo, vol. II.

Chapter 5: 'A Most Famous Feminine Sea Captain'

1. Calendar State Papers (Elizabeth I), vol. 72, no. 39.
2. *Gaelic and Gaelicised Ireland*, p. 73.
3. Lambeth Palace Library, ms. no. 601, p. 111.
4. *Ibid.*
5. SPI 63/170/63.
6. *Hibernia Dominicana*, p. 319.
7. Ordnance Survey Letters, Mayo, vol. I. p.1.
8. Royal Irish Academy, ms. no. Av2 Folio 53A.
9. *Filí agus Filídheacht Chonnacht*, p. 267.

10. *Gaelic and Gaelicised Ireland*, p. 79.
11. *History of the County Mayo*, p. 181.
12. Calendar Carew MSS, vol. II, p. 38.
13. *Ulster Journal of Archaeology*, vol. V, p. 299.
14. Lambeth Palace Library, ms. no 601, p. 101.
15 *Ibid*.
16. SPI 63/19/56.
17 *Ibid.*
18 *Ibid.*
19 SPI 63/19/78.
20. *History of the Town and County of Galway*, p. 86.
21. *The Geraldines*, p. 279.
22. *As Wicked A Woman*, p. 133.
23. Calendar of State Papers (Elizabeth I), vol. CXXII, no. 39.
24. *Ibid.*
25. Calendar of Carew MSS, vol. II, no. 322.
26. SPI 63/172/63.
27. *Ibid.*
28. *Chieftain to Knight*, p. 43.
29. Westport House MSS.
30. *Ibid.*
31. *Ibid.*

Chapter 6: 'Nurse to all Rebellions'

1. Calendar State Papers (Elizabeth I), vol. CLXX, p. 132.
2. Ordnance Survey Letters, Mayo vol. II.
3. *Ibid.*
4. Westport House MSS.
5. *Ibid.*
6. Analecta Hibernia, p. 133.
7. Calendar State Papers (Elizabeth 1), vol. XCIX, p. 424.
8. *Ibid.*
9. *Ibid.*
10. *Annals of the Four Masters*, vol. V, p. 1805.
11. *Ibid.*
12. SPI 63/170/63.
13. *Annals of Loch Cé*, vol. II, p. 459.
14. Westport House MSS.
15. *Ibid.*
16. *Anecdotes and Traditions*, p. 18.
17. Calendar State Papers (Elizabeth I), vol. CLXX, p. 128.
18. *Political Works of Edmund Spenser*, p. 67.

19. Royal Irish Academy, ms. no. AV1, Folio 53A.
20. Titus BXIII, p. 410.
21. MSS Marquis of Salisbury, vol. III, p. 285.
22. SPI 63/170/63.
23. Titus BXIII, p. 236.
24. SPI 63/158/37.
25. SPI 63/170/63.
26. *Ibid.*
28. SPI 63/158/37.
29. *Ibid.*
30. Elizabethan Epic, p. 182.
31. SPI 63/170/63.
32. Calendar of Fiants (Elizabeth I), no. 5173.
33. SPI 63/170/63.

Chapter 7: 'A Notable Traitoress'

1. Westport House MSS.
2. *Ibid.*
3. SPI 63/145/6.
4. Calendar State Papers (Elizabeth I), vol. CLXV, no. 6.
5. Titus BXIII, p. 446.
6. SPI 63/147/35.
7. SPI 63/146/35.
8. Calendar State Papers (Elizabeth I), vol. CLXVII, no. 13.
9. *Ibid.* no. 81.
10. SPI 63/171/18.
11. *Ibid.*
12. SPI 63/158/62.
13. *The Celtic Peoples and Renaissance Europe*, p. 42.
14. Calendar State Papers (Elizabeth I), vol. CLXXI, p. 141.
15. SPI 63/206/92.
16. *History of the County Mayo*, p. 250.
17. *Ibid.*
18. *Irish Pedigrees*, vol. II, p. 675.

Chapter 8: The Meeting of the Two Queens

1. SPI 63/170/204.
2. *Ibid.*
3. SPI 63/171/62.
4. 63/170/44.
5. Dept Celtic Studies, Folklore, Schools MSS no. 4, p. 512.
6. SPI 63/171/37.

7. SPI 63/172/34I.
8. *The Elizabethan Epic*, p. 74.
9. SPI 63/171/44.
10. SPI 63/170/63.
11. Calendar State Papers (Elizabeth I), vol. CLXX, p. 132.
12. *Ibid.*
13. SPI 63/171/62.
14. The Elizabethan Epic, p. 203.
15. *Ibid.* p. 73.
16. *Ibid.* p. 142.
17. *Irish Pedigrees*, vol. II, p. 675.
18. *The Elizabethan Epic*, p. 71.
19. Hatfield House, MSS Marquis of Salisbury, no. CP 169/128.
20. SPI 63/171/44.
21. Hatfield House, no. CP 169/128.
22. SPI 63/170/204.
23. Hatfield House, no. CP 169/128.
24. *Ibid.*
25. SPI 63/171/62.
26. *Ibid.*
27. *Ibid.*
28. SPI 63/171/44.
29. Hatfield House, no. CP 169/128.
30. *Ibid.*

Chapter 9: The End of an Era

1. SPI 63/172/26.
2. *Ibid.*
3. SPI 63/179/81.
4. Calendar State Papers (ElizabethI), vol. CCVI, no. 92.
5. SPI 63/179/36.
6. *Ibid.*
7. *Ibid.*
8. SPI 63/179/35.
9. *Ibid.*
10. SPI 63.179/70.
11. *Ibid.*
12. *Ibid.*
13. *Ibid.*
14. Calendar of Fiants, Elizabeth, no. 5948.
15. *History of Ireland*, vol. III, p. 122.
16. Calendar State Papers (Elizabeth I), 1592-96, preface XXVI.

17. *Life of Hugh Roe O'Donnell*, p. 111.
18. *Scots Mercenary Forces in Ireland*, p. 142.
19. *Annals of the Four Masters*, vol. IV, p. 2013.
20. *Ibid* .
21. Calendar State Papers (Elizabeth I), vol. CC, p. 376.
22. *Ibid.*, vol. CCVIII, p. 436.
23. SPI 63/237/12.

Chapter 10: The Descendants of Granuaile

1. *Chieftain to Knight*, p. 11.
2. Calendar of Carew MSS, vol. III, p. 490.
3. *Ibid.* vol. VIII, p. 136.
4. Galway Archaeological and Historical Society, vol. 11, p. 54.
5. *Funeral Entries Books*, vol. V, p. 147.
6. Lindsay MS, PRO.

Bibliography

1. Manuscript Sources

British Library
Cotton Titus BXIII, VXIII, Papers on Irish affairs, 1559–1602

Department of Celtic Studies, UCD
MSS nos. 86, 202, A229, 693, 838, 1134, 1181, 1206, 1238, 1838, 4844

Howth Castle, Co. Dublin
Gaisford St Lawrence Papers

Genealogical Office, Dublin
MSS nos. 482–5, 699, 165, 155
Funeral Entries Books, vol. 2

Hatfield House, Hertfordshire
Cecil Papers no. 169/128

Lambeth Palace Library
MSS 601, 619

National Library of Ireland
State Papers relating to Ireland (on microfilm, originals in the Public
  Record Office, London)
SP 63/19/56, 186, 63/61/74, 63/72/63, 63/88/34, 63/96/37, 63/145/6, 164,
  63/146/35, 43I, 43II, 43III, 43IV, 148, 63/147/18III, 63/158/37, 62,
  63/170/44, 168, 204, 63/171/18, 37, 44, 62, 65, 81; 63/172/26, 34I,
  63/173/1, 63, 63/179/35, 36, 36I, 38, 70, 75, 77, 62–66, 63/199/66V,
  66VI, 63/200/356, 63/206/20, 63/237/12

Public Record Office, Ireland
Chancery Bills nos. 1.209, R.63, R.65, A.A. 150
Lindsay MS no. 6

Royal Irish Academy, Dublin
MSS nos. AV2 F.53A

Westport House Manuscript Collection, Westport House, Co. Mayo

212 Granuaile: The Life and Times of Grace O'Malley

2. Contemporary Sources

Analecta Hibernia nos., 8, 24, 26.

Annala Rioghachta Éireann. Annals of the Kingdom of Ireland by the Four Masters, from the earliest period to the year 1616, ed. and trans. J. O'Donovan. 7 vols., (Dublin 1851).

Annals of Loch Cé. A Chronicle of Irish Affairs, 1014–1590, ed. W.M. Hennessy, 2 vols. (London, 1871).

Annals of Ulster, ed. B. MacCarthy (Dublin, 1893).

Books of Survey and Distribution, Mayo 1636–1703 (Dublin, 1956).

Camden, W., *Britannia* (London, 1695).

Davis, Sir John, *A Discovery of the True Causes why Ireland was Never Entirely Subdued ...* (London, 1612), Facsimile reprint (Shannon, 1969).

Derrick, J., *The Image of Ireland* (London, 1581), Facsimile reprint (Belfast, 1985).

Hogan, E. ed. *Description of Ireland* (Dublin, 1878).

Hogan, E. and N. MacNeill, eds., *The Walsingham Letterbook*, May 1576 to December 1579 (Dublin, 1959).

Holinshed, R., *Chronicles of England, Scotland and Ireland*, ed. J. Johnson, (London, 1807–8).

Moryson, F., *An Itinerary* (London, 1617), Facsimile edition (Glasgow, 1907–8).

O'Cleary, L., *The Life of Hugh Roe O'Donnell, Prince of Tirconail, 1586–1602* (Dublin, 1893).

O'Donovan, J. ed. and trans. *Leabhar na gCeart. The Book of Rights* (Dublin, 1847).

O'Flaherty, R.A., *Chorographical Description of West Connaught 1684*, (Dublin, 1846).

Perrot, J., *The Chronicles of Ireland 1584–1608*, ed. H. Wood (Dublin, 1933).

Spencer, E., *A View of the Present State of Ireland ... in 1596*, ed. W.I. Renwick (Oxford, 1970).

Stafford, T., *Pacata Hibernia* (London, 1633), ed. S.H. O'Grady (London, 1896).

Calendars and Printed Manuscript Sources

Calendar of the Carew Manuscripts, ed. J.S Brewer and W. Bullen, 6 vols. (London, 1867–73).

Calendar of Cecil Manuscripts, 8 vols. (London, 1883–1899).

Calendar of Fiants of the Reign of Elizabeth, (Dublin, 1877–94).

Calendar of Patent and Close Rolls of Chancery, Elizabeth ed., J.C. Morrin (Dublin, 1862).

Calendar of the Manuscripts of the Marquis of Salisbury (London, 1883–1973).

Calendar of State Papers Relating to Ireland, (London, 1860–1912).

Composition Book of Connaught, ed. A. Freeman (Dublin, 1936).

Sidney State Papers, 1565–70, ed. T. O' Laidhin (Dublin, 1962).

Sidney, Letters and Memorials of State, written and collected by Sir Henry Sidney, Sir Philip Sidney and his brother, Sir Robert Sidney, ed. A. Collins (London, 1746).

Secondary Sources

Anthology Hibernica, vol. II (Dublin, 1793).

Bagwell, R., *Ireland under the Tudors*, 3 vols. (London, 1885–90).

Bagwell, R., *Ireland under the Stuarts*, 3 vols. (London, 1909–16).

Ball, F., *Howth and its Owners* (Dublin, 1917).

Beckett, J.C. *The Making of Modern Ireland* (London, 1966).

Black, C., *Pirates of the West Indies* (Cambridge, 1989).

Black, J.B., *The Reign of Elizabeth, 1558–1603* (Oxford, 1959).

Blackwell, M., *Ships in Early Irish History* (Co. Clare, 1992).

Butler, W.F.T., *Confiscation in Irish History* (1917)

Byrne, M., *Ireland Under Elizabeth* (Dublin, 1903)

Callwell, J., *Old Irish Life* (London, 1912).

Canny, N., *The Elizabethan Conquest. A Pattern Established, 1565–76* (1976).

Chambers, A., *Chieftain to Knight. Tibbott-ne-Long Bourke, Viscount Mayo, 1567–1629* (Dublin, 1983).

Chambers, A., *As Wicked A Woman, Eleanor Countess of Desmond, 1545–1638* (Dublin, 1989).

Cordingly, D., *Life Among the Pirates* (UK, 1995).

Corkery, D., *The Hidden Ireland* (Dublin, 1979).

Dutton, R., *English Court Life* (London, 1963).

Ellis, S.G., *Tudor Ireland* (London, 1985).

Fallon, N., *The Armada in Ireland* (London, 1978).

Falls, C., *Elizabeth's Irish Wars* (London, 1950).

Fitzgerald, B., *The Geraldines, 1169–1601* (London, 1951).

Hardiman, J., *History of the Town and County of Galway* (Dublin, 1920).

Hardiman, J., *Irish Minstrelsy*, vol. II (London, 1831).

Ireland, J. de Courcy, *Ireland and the Irish in Maritime History* (Dublin, 1986).

Joyce, P., *Social History of Ancient Ireland* (Dublin, 1913).

Knox, H.T., *History of the County Mayo* (Dublin, 1908).

Leask, H.G., *Irish Castles and Castellated Houses* (Dundalk, 1972).

Loades, D., *The Tudor Court* (London, 1992).

McCalmont, R.F., *Memories of the Binghams* (London, 1915).

McClintock, H., *Irish and Highland Dress* (Dundalk, 1950).

McClintock, H., *Handbook of Old Irish Dress* (Dundalk, 1958).

McCoy, Hayes, G., *Scots Mercenary Forces in Ireland, 1565–1607* (Dublin, 1937).

Mac Lysaght, E., *Irish Life in the 17th Century* (Cork, 1939).

MacCurtain, M., *Tudor and Stuart Ireland* (Dublin, 1972).

MacCurtain, M., O'Dowd, M., eds., *Women in Early Modern Ireland* (Dublin, 1991).

Mason, T., *The Islands of Ireland* (London, 1936).

Maxwell, C., *The Stranger in Ireland* (London, 1934).

Moody, T., Martin, F., Byrnes, F., eds. *A New History of Ireland*, Vol III (Oxford, 1976).

Neale, J., *Elizabeth I and her Parliaments, 1584–1601* (London, 1958).

Nicholls, K., *Gaelic and Gaelicised Ireland in the Middle Ages* (Dublin, 1972).

O'Brien, G., *Economic History of Ireland in the 17th Century* (Dublin, 1919).

O'Faolain, S., *The Great O'Neill* (London, 1950).

O'Hart, J., *Irish Pedigrees* (New York, 1916).

Ó Raghallaigh, T., *Filí agus Filídheacht Chonnacht* (Dublin, 1938).

Otway, C., *A Tour of Connaught* (Dublin, 1839).

Praeger, R.L., *The Way That I Went* (London, 1937).

Prockter, A., Taylor, R., *The A to Z of Elizabethan London* (London 1979).

Ridley, J., *Henry VIII* (London, 1984).

Smith, L.B., *The Elizabethan Epic* (London, 1966).

Stanley, J., ed. *Bold in Her Breeches* (London, 1995).

Thackeray, W.M., *The Irish Sketch Book* (London, 1902).

Thomas, D.A., *The Illustrated Armada Handbook* (London, 1988).

Townsend, J.H., *Buccaneer Queen* (London, 1902).

Walsh, M. Kerney, *Destruction by Peace* (Armagh, 1986).

Westropp, T., *Clare Island Survey* (Dublin, 1911).

Wilson, P., *The Beginnings of Modern Ireland* (Dublin, 1912).

Journals and Articles

Dublin University Magazine, vol LIII (1959).

Folklore, vol. XXVIII, no. 4.

Galway Archaeological and Historical Society, vols. I–VII, XVIII.

Irish Genealogist, vol. I.

Irish Sword, vol. I.

Kerry Archaeological Society, vol. VIII (1975).

Lord of the Isles Voyage Brochure (1993).

Nichols, K., 'Land, Law and Society in Sixteenth Century Ireland' O'Donnell Lecture (UCC, 1976).

Ó Morain, P., 'Five Hundred Years in the History of Murrisk Abbey' (*Mayo News*, 7 & 14 September 1975).

Ordnance Survey. *Letters Relating to the County of Mayo*, vols. I, II, ed. John O'Donovan (Dublin, 1862).

Ordnance Survey. *Letters relating to the Country of Galway* ed. John O'Donovan (Dublin, 1862).

Proceedings of the Royal Irish Academy, vol. 36.

Revue Celtique, vol. XLIX.

Ulster Journal of Archaeology, vols. II, IV, V, VIII.

Index